6.8.67.

THE PUPPET THEATRE

of the Modern World

THE PUPPET THEATRE

of the Modern World

An International Presentation in Word and Picture

Compiled by an Editorial Board of
UNION INTERNATIONALE
DES MARIONNETTES
under the Chairmanship of
MARGARETA NICULESCU

Translated by
EWALD OSERS & ELIZABETH STRICK

GEORGE G. HARRAP & CO. LTD
London   Toronto   Wellington   Sydney

First published in Great Britain 1967

by GEORGE G. HARRAP & CO. LTD

182 High Holborn, London, W.C.1

Copyright by Henschelverlag

Kunst und Gesellschaft, Berlin 1965

English translation © *George G. Harrap & Co. Ltd* 1967

PRINTED IN EAST GERMANY BY FORTSCHRITT, ERFURT

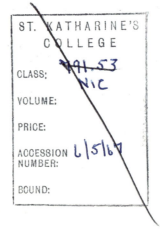

Preface

by Margareta Niculescu

Rumanian. Director of the "Tandarica" Theatre, Bucharest, the leading Rumanian puppet theatre and one of the most interesting in Europe. It has twice obtained the principal award at the International Puppet Festival at Bucharest.

To modern man, moving ceaselessly in a world peopled by the creations of his detached intellect, the puppet remains an expression of his yearning for magic and poetry. Itself in a state of continuous change, it lends form to the changing character of man.

Over the last few years that little creature of cloth and cardboard, whose mystery time and again we try to unravel, has clearly acquired more matter-of-factness without, on the other hand, losing its naïveté; it has become more subtle without forfeiting its popular character, and more poetic without losing its spiritual substance.

What changes will puppetry—that age-old art whose means have already been transformed so fundamentally—undergo in the future? Is it perhaps on the threshold of a new era, or will it develop into that total work of art predicted by our idealists, when all branches of art will fuse into a single entirely individual art category?

The international editorial board of this book, production of which was encouraged by the UNIMA Praesidium, hopes in this way to promote a first symposium to discuss this and other topical questions of puppetry. We therefore approached all our colleagues with the request to support our project. The articles submitted to us have been arranged around specific themes, thus preserving the full independence of each contribution.

The illustrations are arranged like a journey across the continents–enabling us to gain an overall view, to learn more about one another, and to allow others to make our acquaintance. We hope that we may have succeeded for the first time in providing a general prospectus of the world of puppetry today, making provision for the most varied traditions and forms, an artistic universe embracing different views of the world and of art. Thus the traditional classical line and contemporary experiments, the daring novelty of new forms, may co-exist one alongside the other.

A testimony to an age in transition, the present book has endeavoured to bear in mind the worldwide character of our ideas.

To all those who have so obligingly met our requests and contributed to the success of our journey we express our sincere thanks.

Tradition and the Present Day

by Jan Malík

Czech. Secretary-General of UNIMA and director of one of the leading puppet theatres in Prague. Dr Malík has devoted a great part of his life, both before and after the war, to encouraging international friendship and co-operation among puppeteers.

For many centuries, especially in Europe, the history of the puppet theatre–in particular, of its most wide-spread form, the marionette theatre–represented a kind of miniature edition of the live theatre, as much in repertoire as in production and stage design. Indeed, to this day the most common type of marionette theatre is none other than a small-scale edition of the human theatre of the Baroque, and to this day we find among marionette operators a tendency to make their puppets as close as possible to human reality.

Against this traditional, or rather conservative and fundamentally dubious, interpretation of the puppet theatre the first attempts at reform appeared around the turn of the nineteenth and twentieth centuries; instinctive at first rather than programmatic, they aimed at establishing the autonomy of the puppet theatre and winning recognition for its own artistic rules.

It is significant that this process should be found first of all in those countries which had a relatively long tradition of puppetry–especially marionettes–and where a decline in the strictly traditional and hence less and less viable forms of puppetry had been plainly noticeable over a period of years. Thus it happened that, chiefly in the so-called classical countries of European puppetry, such as Italy, France, and the region embracing present-day Germany, Austria, and Czecho-slovakia, a number of artistically conscious and sometimes entirely exclusive puppet theatres came into being, such as that of Papa Schmid and Pocci in Munich, which opened in 1858, while in the meantime the old marionette tradition continued to survive in hundreds of small and very small theatres.

As far as amateur puppet theatres were concerned, their strict adherence to tradition was marked far more in their puppets, stage sets, and stage technique than in their repertoire or production, where certain reforms did at times appear, especially in the use of better texts, in the increased attention paid to fairy-tale themes, and in a tendency towards greater linguistic purity and less bombastic declamation. In contrast, the commercial touring marionette theatres clung to tradition mainly in the worst sense–preserving outdated mannerisms, bad taste, and often deliberate coarseness, all usually without any talent on the part of the puppeteers, since an itinerant marionette theatre was simply an inherited family business like any other. The fact that these dubious productions continued to survive between the two wars is due principally to an uncritical conservatism which regarded them as a popular manifestation of a folklore tradition and which, in consequence, was responsible for the growing prejudice against puppetry among the adult public. There were also certain questionable and hardly excusable "social considerations". They are the reason why, at a time when a healthy development in the 'big' theatre had long since swept away the pseudo art of the penny gaff–formerly such a blot on the escutcheon of the itinerant disciples of the theatrical muse–in the marionette theatre a pseudo art was still retarding and often positively frustrating the development of a contemporary art of puppetry by offering to the broad masses of an ill-informed public either a caricature of puppetry tradition or at best a kind of anachronistic performance that belonged to the museum.

But although in a museum we may show great interest in a primitive wooden plough without a metal ploughshare, we would never dream of advocating its practical use "for the sake of ancient folk tradition". We may like the picturesque appearance of a timber-built cottage, but when we come to choose our own weekend chalet we shall probably prefer a more modern and, above all, a more hygienic type of building. Taking examples from the theatre itself, if we could bring back David Garrick, Edmund Kean, Tommaso Salvini, Sarah Bernhardt, or Eleonora Duse and see them play their most famous parts in what by now has become a classical repertoire, there is little doubt that we would cruelly destroy the halo of glory which surrounds these giants of the stage, these men and women who in their own day were certainly actors of genius. We need only think of the almost invariably comical impression produced by former idols of the silver screen whenever an old film tragedy is shown to today's audiences. Of course, we can see old stills or films, or listen to old gramophone records of long-dead actors, with appreciation and respect, just as we may applaud the achievements of a silent film or an early talkie–but that is something entirely different. Here we are dealing with a historical document, with a museum piece, with something from the archives. We supplement our visual or acoustic experience by the fullest possible reconstruction of the period in question; we do not transfer the historical work into an alien and therefore grotesquely contrasting present, but accept every achievement and each personality deliberately and without mystique as a historical phenomenon, as a piece of the past, socially valid in its own day but today meaningful only in its historical context and relationships.

We do not, of course, wish to rule out exceptions or deny that something may come down to us which, though an evident anachronism, has nevertheless preserved pure traditional characteristics well over a hundred years old. Indeed, there are several such examples in the history of contemporary puppetry. One of them is the popular Russian operator of marionettes and glove puppets, Ivan Afinogenovich Zaitsev (1863–1936), who was honoured with the title Meritorious Artist of the USSR and spent the last years of his life as a privileged member of the State Central Puppet Theatre directed by S. V. Obraztsov in Moscow. Living quietly, Zaitsev kept his stock of marionettes and properties intact and only occasionally showed his puppets in performances intended as illustrations of cultural history. Obraztsov's theatre, in addition to many other collectors' items in its museum, possessed Zaitsev's string, glove, and variety-show puppets which this great artist in the popular tradition used to operate in the authentic style and with such incomparable skill.

As for recording the ancient tradition of puppetry–a late starter compared with others in the fields of folklore study–this was for many decades confined to written records and laboriously salvaged manuscripts. Pictorial records depended on the testimony of painters and photographers. More recently valuable services have been rendered by gramophone records and films, and more recently still by sound films and tape recordings.

Although these records today are still more often the domain of the ethnographer and philologist rather than the theatrical scholar, one must at least welcome the fact that the collected body of these records of a vanishing tradition is growing apace. Thus we have some very good sound films today of the famous traditional Japanese Bunraku-Za in Osaka, a whole series of puppet films from Indonesia, an excellent film from India, a sound film record of the Karagöz shadow plays from Greece, etc. In Czechoslovakia the voices of the oldest marionette operators were preserved on gramophone records in 1947 in typical roles from the traditional repertoire, and more recently, in 1959, a 16-millimetre documentary film was made, with the support of the Theatre Institute, of the grand old man of Czech puppetry, Tomáš Dubský (born 1874), doing a traditional play from his repertoire, Mácháček's *Bridegrooms*.

Invaluable work in the preservation and sometimes even the production of such documents has been done by various specialized museums, such as the Municipal Puppet Theatre Collection in Munich, the State Puppet Theatre Collection in Dresden, the puppetry collections of the Theatre Institute in Cologne, the International Marionette Museum in Lyons, the puppetry departments of the national or municipal museums in Brussels, Liège, Antwerp, and Prague, a number of outstanding collections in the United States, and elsewhere. Nor should we forget the hundreds of private collectors, often specializing in a particular aspect of puppetry; their collections and archives, frequently built up by a lifetime's efforts, deserve to be concentrated systematically, and, more important still, in good time, for our public collections.

After this digression—a somewhat sketchy one, since the scope of this article does not permit us to deal with this subject in detail—it should be pointed out that tradition in its true, widest, and deepest social meaning is not a museum piece. The difficulty, of course, is that we are often unable to decide whether a particular puppet show should be viewed as a mere anachronism, as a non-creative and mechanically traditional replica, as a sterile specimen, a sideshow attraction, a cultural antique, or as the gift of a happy chance which enables us to see a performance representing the spontaneous reincarnation of a long-concluded phase of development, complete with all its characteristics. To attempt a rigid classification into dead cultural fossils on the one hand and carefully preserved survivals on the other is of little value, since the transition from the one to the other takes place gradually and is marked by a whole series of individual characteristics, specific causes, and subtle relationships. Thus, a surprisingly fierce dispute broke out quite recently on whether the old-established marionette theatre in Munich should be liquidated or not, and the traditional Bunraku-Za in Osaka went through a crisis at almost exactly the same time.

There are even more complicated and more delicate questions. What, for instance, is to become of the original Poesje survivors in Antwerp, or of its sister establishment in Liège, or of the Toone Theatre in Brussels, whose present principal Toone VI—actually Pierre Welleman (born 1892)—is trying to meet his theatre's difficulties by the gradual sale of his stock?

How is one to judge the spirited achievements of Henrik Kemény (born 1925), now a member of the Budapest National Puppet Theatre, who from time to time performs glove-puppet comedies in the spirit and style of his age-old family tradition? Where should one place the typical action pattern of the Punch and Judy shows, and can one judge them by today's yardsticks? What is one to make of all their present-day English variants and interpreters, headed by the irresist-ible Percy Press (born 1902)? And still on the subject of British specialities, how is one to explain the great popularity of the "model theatres", those printed miniature theatres with their flat paper figures, old-fashioned proscenium arches, backdrops, and flats (and even the reprints of the old texts as still published by the London firm of Benjamin Pollock), a peculiarity which we know also from Denmark? And why does the Sicilian Marionette Theatre with its massive top-heavy wire puppets, with its traditional repertoire based on themes from the Crusades and its noisy bombast, stubbornly continue to attract audiences? Then there is the Hänneschen Theater in Cologne (founded in 1802 by Christoph Winter) with its ancient romantic repertoire and its primitive rod-puppet technique. This theatre still plays in its original style on a stage which has formally preserved its traditional spatial arrangement even though the décor is now clearly the work of an experienced stage artist and the space behind the scenes is equipped with overhead pulleys and other technical facilities, though the professional actors are reinforced by a tape recorder with amplifiers and loudspeakers and the piano has an elaborate multi-register electronic sound apparatus. Are we to recognize this theatre as a cultural history reserve and justify its modernized equipment behind the scenes by pointing out that telegraph offices, service stations, and other aspects of present-day civilization are found even in nature reserves?

It cannot be denied that the majority of these anachronistic productions are being kept alive partly—often indeed mainly—as a tourist attraction. But this does not explain the continuing spontaneous and virtually nation-wide popularity of traditional English Punch and Judy shows, nor the fact that the Hänneschen Theater in Cologne is playing almost daily not only to adult audiences but, moreover, almost exclusively to local fans of this traditionally-minded genre.

To solve a specialized problem responsibly and to avoid arriving at wrong conclusions, sentiment must be excluded from our analysis and arguments. Like any other artistic agency the theatre performs a social function and can be viewed as an art form only if it is closely linked to the present day.

To play a traditional repertoire, including classical authors, is not only possible but indeed necessary—always provided that our production of the classical play has something useful and valid to say to modern audiences, and in the language of today. On no account should we attempt to produce Shakespeare under the conditions and in the style of the Elizabethan stage; any such attempt would produce not a piece of live theatre but a museum-type reconstruction. Naturally, such a reconstruction might cause a sensation—as, for instance, Reinhardt's famous production of *The Miracle*—but it would be a production of ephemeral fame and without creative value for the future.

The question of tradition in the puppet theatre is customarily linked with the existence of its principal comic character. Whereas the big theatre—whose modern age began as early as the turn of the eighteenth and nineteenth centuries—has long since got over this problem, it has to this day remained topical in the puppet theatre of those countries where the old traditional habits and the influence of folklore theatre have survived. Besides—and this should be remembered—such a principal comic figure is always a type, and we know that a system of types is ideally appropriate to the puppetry repertoire.

From the symbolical burning of the Hanswurst figure, the traditional German clown, by the German actress and theatrical manageress Friederike Caroline Neuber (1697–1760) in the year 1737 it was over a century before the Hanswurst in all its shapes had really vanished from the big stage. It is therefore not surprising that his puppet version, under the name of Kasperl (with such variants as Staberl, Jackerl, Lipperl, Thaddädl, Larifari, etc.), has proved himself an even more stubborn survivor. Whether these principal comic types owe their origin and development to native roots alone or whether they have grown from dormant roots due to a chance impulse from abroad—to speak of imported types would be a very superficial and inaccurate interpretation—each one of them soon assumed original national traits. Most of them suggested in their very names that, as heroes of the popular puppet comedy, they were not only the darlings but also the children of the people, symbols of the people's unceasing struggle for their daily bread and their bare existence.

Descending from a long pedigree which includes the ancient Roman "Mimus albus", Maccus and Centunculus (the ancestors of Pierrot and Harlequin), Italy produced Pulcinella and his regional twin brothers Gianduja and Gerolamo, France produced Polichinelle and (in Lyons) Guignol, Spain Don Christóbal de Polichinel, England Punch and the Anglo-Saxon John Pickle Herring, Holland Jan Klaassen, Belgium Tchantchès, Switzerland Hans Joggeli, Denmark Mester Jakel, Bohemia Pimperle and later Kašpárek, and Russia Petroushka Farnos—Krasny Nos (Red Nose) also known as Petr Ivanovich Uksukov, or Samovarov, or Vanka Ratutay and the Ukrainian Vanka Rutyutyu; elsewhere we have the Bulgarian Pencho, the Hungarian Paprika Jancsi, the Rumanian Vasilache, the Turkish-Arabian Karagöz (Black Eye) and his Greek double Karankiósés, the Armenian-Persian Palwan-Katchal (Giant Bald-Head) or Karapet, the Indian Vidushaka, the Indonesian Semar, etc.—in short, a truly unending gallery of characters which is being added to through new discoveries.

There is no denying that, hand in hand with the renaissance of the puppetry movement, the last half-century witnessed nearly everywhere a decline in the once universal popularity of these comic types. The usual process is that the traditional jesters of the puppet stage first adapt themselves to the greatly changed conditions and requirements, enlarging their artistic means of expression, and sometimes even abandoning the features and clothes associated with them from time immemorial. From there it is only one step to their complete disappearance; the ancient clowns of the puppet stage, the last heirs of the Commedia dell'arte, are giving way in certain countries to new comic types bearing different names. And finally these stereotyped comic characters disappear from the stage altogether, to make room for the new heroes. The central type, and even the principal comic type, is no longer the comic character of the old plays—i. e., a character deliberately introduced into the plot to provide a more or less active factor in the comedy, a reasoning chorus in the tragedy, or just a light-hearted commentator on the action. The new central type is developing organically from the requirements, character, and style of each play which invests its heroes, like all other characters, with an ever-new form, with new characteristics, a new function in the plot, and, moreover, the chance of further development in the course of the play.

What Punch (together with his numerous relations) has done for us, as much as for the old-time puppeteer, is to make us realize the importance of a type, in particular for the puppet theatre and its repertoire. Even if Punch and some of his twin brothers one day were to disappear altogether, the puppet theatre of types would live on for ever. This is a process taking place quite spontaneously; it is purely a symptom of objective development and by no means the result of conscious, let alone decreed, reform.

Every tradition becomes an obstacle, a millstone, the moment it has lost its social and period-determined justification. Ever since Maeterlinck's "Puppet Dramas", the puppet theatre in general had come to the end of the period that was marked by the action of the traditional comic type in each play. Alongside formal experiments and innovations it began, especially after the Second World War, to create its own repertoire for the first time in its history—a specific puppet-type repertoire unrestricted by traditional convention.

The history of the past few decades testifies that this new phase is progressing organically. When the Russian Petroushka had come to the end of his social role in 1917 it was of no avail to him that he continued to live on for many years, especially on the propaganda stage, nor that at the first Congress of Soviet Writers in 1935 Maxim Gorky defended his traditional value and significance with spirit, much wit, and great power of persuasion, nor even that to this day he is speaking to child readers in the delightful small plays, published in book form, of Samuil Marshak. Petroushka's chapter in history was virtually closed from the moment when the new Russian puppet play began to develop, when a new puppetry repertoire was created in the same way and at the same level as that enjoyed by the big theatre. Similarly, Kašpárek, until then the indispensable chief character of the Czech marionette

play, disappeared from the stage in the first years after the Second World War, and he has stayed off it despite the fact that attempts were made in the fifties—moreover, with semi-official encouragement—to revive his tradition. To Czech children today Kašpárek is a literary concept rather than a character on the stage; in his stead the contemporary Czech puppetry repertoire has gained a whole string of new puppet heroes and is gaining more all the time.

The viability of the comic types of the puppet stage, in their most popular and artistically most mature characters, has always been determined by the artistic style and creative individuality of their interpreters. Thus, ever since 1921 when the German Hartenstein (later renamed "Hohnsteiner") glove-puppet theatre was founded, the Kasperl created and superbly interpreted by the dramatist Max Jacob (born 1888) has grown to classical stature—and for this very reason the heirs of the Hohnsteiner tradition have no wish to pay tribute to their creator by simple imitation, however accomplished, but instead are trying to impress on the theatre their own stamp, at first in the repertoire and the conception of stage production, and increasingly also in a different interpretation of the leading character. Sooner or later even the famous Hohnsteiner Kasperl will change in many different ways and be absorbed into a number of new central hero types.

In Czechoslovakia the famous comic pair of marionettes, Father Špejbl and his little son Hurvínek, gained world fame because their creator or co-creator, vocal interpreter and occasional operator, the National Prize Winner Josef Skupa (1892–1957), was a puppeteer of genius. Not surprisingly, after Skupa's death his theatre was faced with the problem of how the future theatrical existence of these two marionettes, indissolubly connected as they were with the personality and unique interpretative skill of their creator, could be artistically justified. For much the same reason, Carl Schröder (born 1904), the outstanding German glove-puppet operator and a man of exceptional creative gifts, deliberately switched over in some of the last plays of his stage career to a repertoire without a Kasperl figure, and as a librettist, scenario writer, puppet designer, and producer of outstanding puppet films in the Dresden DEFA studios continued to develop the art of glove puppetry in a new medium—in repertoire and style combining both the best German and his own personal traditions, but free from all antiquarian and hence socially meaningless trappings.

National traditions of puppetry often have a fertilizing and inspiring effect beyond the frontiers of their native countries, and not only in respect of their principal comic types. The manifold forms and results of such influences can be illustrated by means of a few significant examples.

A chance encounter with examples of Javanese marionette art in a Dutch museum induced Professor Richard Teschner of Vienna to stage, first of all, a reconstruction of a Javanese puppet play with original Javanese figures of the Wajang-Golek type. Later he used the same characters in textual adaptations of his own, and finally he took over from his Javanese models only the basic technical principle and thus began to create his own, artistically entirely original and technically improved rod puppets, for which he wrote pantomime libretti and even composed the music for instruments of his own design.

The French glove-puppet operator Jean-Loup Temporal (born 1921) became fully familiar even as a child with the stage practice and style of his father, Marcel Temporal. Later —by then a professional puppeteer—he passed through the practical school of Max Jacob, the German glove-puppet operator, and today he is in the top rank of the French hand-puppet theatre, not only because of his talent, but also because he has succeeded in applying the experience and ideas gained in Jacob's Hohnsteiner theatre to the development of his own personal style—a style of compelling charm, wit, and lyricism, marked by a very individual direction and stage design.

The age-old trick known even to our grandparents' generation from the performances of drawing-room conjurers was utilized by the French puppeteer Georges Lafaye for his 'black theatre', in which the interplay of objects and symbols is inspired with poetic life. His example led to a few experiments at the Špejbl and Hurvínek Theatre in Prague, which were continued particularly by Jiří Srnec, whose 'black thea-

tre' can already look back on a number of impressive successes abroad. Unfortunately the tempting possibilities of exporting these attractive and effective pantomimes have resulted in two more 'black theatres' being set up in Prague, and there is now a danger that this lively and modern, but basically gimmicky genre may become a superficial fashion. However, the 'black theatre' is growing increasingly popular also among amateurs and has now even begun to create its own special repertoire.

The tradition of the Chinese shadow play, which spread to Europe during the Chinoiserie fashion of the rococo period, triggered off a large-scale development of this art in most civilized countries, even though Europe preferred a different form as far as technique is concerned. The original Chinese shadow-play technique has been revived only in the original "San mei hua pan" theatre in which the German theatrical scholar Dr Max Bührmann (born 1904) has been performing German translations of traditional Chinese shadow plays with original Chinese figures and original Chinese music since 1951. While this aspect of Bührmann's many-sided activity is chiefly of specialized educational and—in the best sense of the word— propaganda character, the Dresden writer and dramatist Fritz Gay (born 1907) took over merely the Chinese technique and basic stylistic repertoire of the Oriental model for his theatre "Die Schatten". It is his merit to have enriched German puppetry with his original shadow stage, both by the poetic value of his texts and by his sensitive direction and artistic standards.

Earlier historical contacts and mutual influences of the various national traditions of puppetry are exceedingly difficult to discover and prove. There is, for instance, a very obvious connection between the traditional marionette cycles in Sicily and the Belgian Poesje marionettes. Similarly, between the portable sack-shaped glove-puppet box we know from a drawing in the travel diary of the Holstein diplomat Adam Olearius who journeyed in Russia in 1636 and the same system known to us from Central Asia; undoubtedly these go back to Chinese models. On the other hand, the unique character of the Hänneschen Theater in Cologne suggests that here we have the survival of an echo of East European puppetry tradition such as is embodied, for instance, in the Ukrainian "Vertyep", in the Polish "Szopka" or in the Czech "Jesle" (traditional Christmas crib plays).

To promote interest in the dying or already defunct traditional forms of puppetry an international research centre, CIPEMAT (Centre International pour les Études des Marionnettes Traditionnelles), was set up in Liège in 1958. Unfortunately, there have been no developments since this constituent meeting, as no money has been available for further work.

In conclusion here are a few observations on two subjects which are connected, on the one hand, with the development of national puppetry traditions and, on the other, with the entire problem of their cross-fertilization in present conditions.

Spring 1957 marked the beginning of a series of international puppetry festivals, organized mostly in collaboration with UNIMA or under its patronage. These festivals–and this is true also of the national festivals–are usually combined with exhibitions; and these have shown that even countries which had been thought to have no puppetry tradition at all (such as Poland, Rumania, Hungary, Yugoslavia, and others) are sending to these events a surprising wealth of material testifying to their hitherto unknown or even disputed history of puppetry. The collections brought together for such exhibitions would be eminently suitable to form the nuclei of future national puppetry museums.

The international festivals, moreover, provide the most economical opportunity for gaining information on the whole subject. In the course of a few days an expert can acquaint himself with at least the main trends of contemporary puppetry and gain new knowledge and ideas on a scale, both in breadth and depth, that would have been impossible even on a twelve months' study trip to all the corners of the globe. Against these undoubtedly very positive aspects of the festivals must unfortunately also be set a number of negative or at least questionable ones. It is a fact that at these grand reviews of puppetry certain theatres perform not typical exam-ples of their everyday work, but special productions devised for these great occasions. These performances are aimed, almost invariably, at a festival public and the jury–*i. e.*, at an adult and international public–whereas at home they play exclusively, or overwhelmingly, to child audiences. They thus disregard the old truth that the greatest international effect is produced by that art which manifests its national traits in the purest form. They deny their national stylistic note and are only too ready to adapt themselves to 'fashionable' trends. For their professional colleagues in the puppet theatre these festival events are therefore not a source of information or creative inspiration, but frequently an inducement to imitation, to a chase after 'fashion', to a pseudo avant-garde formalism and snobbery, and sometimes even plagiarism.

Similar problems are raised by guest performances in foreign countries. In an endeavour to make things as easy as possible for an audience speaking a different language, theatres tend to choose programmes in which the purely visual side predominates–most frequently musicals, ballet or variety programmes, and more recently also pantomime. There is, of course, no objection to such a choice, but merely for the sake of facile success one should not scrap what, even on the puppet stage, is ultimately the indispensable substance of all theatre–the dramatic text. Naturally, to export a production which rests primarily on the dramatic text is a rather complicated business, and therefore some theatres resort to practices which must give rise to serious critical reservations. While a live theatrical company on tour abroad usually contents itself with an informative article in the printed programme or with a spoken introduction to the play–if necessary, to each act–the puppet theatres often go further. They accompany the softly spoken original text with a synchronized translation played at full volume, or else–and this is an even more controversial solution–they render the original text, either direct or on tape recording, in the foreign language. Sometimes we find the extreme case of the actors memorizing the foreign-language text by ear and speaking their part as a kind of "canned sound-track" without even knowing the foreign language in question.

In these cases the bounds of true art have almost certainly been seriously transgressed and the puppet shows have got into the realm of mere technical brilliance. We would be not only surprised but positively shocked if, for instance, an English theatrical company on tour in, say, Greece attempted to play their parts by speaking their words in Greek. After all, we are not interested in whether or how well a group of Finnish actors masters the Spanish language, but a Spanish audience is likely to be interested in seeing and hearing those Finnish actors acting in their own native tongue. Why then should the interpretation of a dramatic text by a puppet theatre be subject to less stringent rules?

Study trips similarly have their positive and negative side. We know the perpetual difficulties which confront a country which has been too anxious to adopt ready-made foreign models; we know how many years such countries had to spend in sterile imitative endeavour and how ready they have been at times to underrate or even deny their own native traditional values. Think of the damage done, especially in the theatre and hence also in puppetry, by so-called 'Europeanization' in countries with a centuries-old and mature stage culture such as China, Japan, India, Vietnam, etc. A study trip demands not only expert qualifications but also a measure of tact, respect, and profound knowledge on the part of the traveller, and it demands critical attention and healthy national pride on the part of those who are the objects of the study. If today we are striving to bring about an extension and a deepening of international relations (and we are proud to think that puppetry is playing an important part in the realization of this humanitarian programme), this does not mean that we wish to deny, let alone to liquidate, that which forms the nutritive soil of all creative artistic achievement—a country's national tradition, its national handwriting, its national style—in order to propagate some levelling cosmopolitanism.

Contemporary
Puppetry

Opinions and Assessments

Some Considerations on the Puppet Theatre

by Sergei Obraztsov

Russian. Director of the State Central Puppet Theatre, Moscow. Obraztsov is perhaps the most famous puppet artist in the world today; his theatre has toured all over the world, including Great Britain (Edinburgh Festival, 1965) and the United States. His use of rod puppets has influenced an entire generation of puppeteers, especially in Eastern Europe.

The puppet theatre is among the earliest types of spectacle; it may even be the oldest. One thing is certain: it is the one which has been least studied.

The puppet theatre of today can be considered as a junction, a peak where the secular traditions of spectacle in China, Japan, India, Indo-China, and Indonesia meet and blend.

One can safely state that this is one of the most precious of all traditions, and one of the most underrated.

The history of the puppet theatre is a wonderful story of the uninterrupted progress of a spectacle which has—especially when it is compared with other forms of popular art—an unbelievable capacity for international diffusion.

If a universal history of the puppet theatre were written, it would read like a fascinating science-fiction novel in which the gods turned into puppets and the puppets into gods. Puppets have been worshipped, anathematized, even publicly burned. Puppeteers have been despised, treated as the lowest form of life, and at the same time monuments have been raised to them. The police and the Church have forbidden puppets to be shown in the streets, while poets have sung them in their verses.

Puppets have crossed deserts, mountains, and seas, they have travelled through many lands, and in the course of these travels Karagöz, the ridiculous and ugly Turk, has become, imperceptibly and without losing any of his external characteristics, the Greek puppet Karankiósés, who beats the Turks under the flags of Alexander the Great. With the puppet Pulcinella, from Italy, the story is the same: without changing his face or his costume, he has had several changes of nationality. He becomes Polichinelle in France, Punch in England, and Petroushka, one hundred per cent Russian, in Russia.

I should be very happy to read a history of the puppet theatre, in order to learn of all the merits that men see in it and to learn to respect it still more. Who knows, perhaps it is these very merits that make me love it so much.

But no, that is not why I love it, for I know that none of these merits are what gives the art its universal passport in the world of today. I am not a theorist or a historian of the theatre. I do not live in the past; I live firmly in the present. If I am often transported with enthusiasm for the great traditions of the art, it is because they are so many messengers from nameless geniuses, because the finished form, polished by the centuries, is always one of pure beauty. But I never forget that it is the beauty of a sarcophagus concealing a mummy. Deep-rooted traditions are interesting, but they are passports to the past, not tickets to the future.

An elaborate family tree is necessary for aristocrats to justify their titles and for dogs to complete their pedigrees. But the man who goes to a museum and studies the catalogue and not the pictures will understand nothing about painting.

No, I do not love the puppet theatre for its catalogue of merits—a catalogue which in any case has yet to be compiled.

Why, then? Is it really needed? We must not forget how many people think it is not worth taking seriously, that those who study it are wasting their time. Take opera, for instance: that is something quite different, something solid. Battistini, Caruso, Chaliapin. The same applies to ballet. But the puppet theatre? A children's entertainment, on the same level as toys and sweets.

Are these people right? Let us put our memory to work.

The puppet theatre? Two sentimental old women who make a couple of puppets with the help of a few bits of rag and perform little plays made up by themselves. The two ladies are very endearing, but the puppets are bad and the plays ridiculous.

The puppet theatre? A revival of the popular theatre, the origin of Guignol, and Punch, all sorts of historical reminiscences and even a laudatory chronicle. All very well, but plays of this kind provoke more yawns than applause.

The puppet theatre? An exercise for intellectual snobs: a bit of surrealism, a bit of mysticism, a spot of twopenny-halfpenny philosophy. It impresses the producer's wife, the puppeteer's brother, the occasional patron of the arts. And it gives wonderful opportunities for feeling one is a genius.

So there are good reasons for being disgusted by the puppet theatre! But we must not get carried away by our righteous indignation.

Do sentimental old women of both sexes thrive only in the puppet theatre? There are enough of them in all the arts. They exist in the field of poetry, of painting, everywhere you can think of. Besides, they are not the only ones who produce trash. Look in the windows of the souvenir shops in Venice, Rome, Paris, Cairo. Horrible! But luckily the plaster, glass, and plastic Coliseums, gondolas, Venuses, Nefertitis, and Arcs de Triomphe cannot destroy the sublime beauty of the works which inspired the manufacturers to produce their imitations.

Similarly, the pseudo-scientific ideas of restorers of classical art do not exist only in the heads of those who try to revive Guignol or Karagöz. The same ideas turn up in the minds of architects, painters, or producers in the 'human' theatre who imitate now the Commedia dell'arte, now Shakespeare's Globe, and now the theatre of the old travelling players.

For there are many people who like to see life with others' eyes and to depict it through an art which is not their own; but can infantile imitations of children's art destroy the beauty of drawings by real children? People sweat blood trying to force wood and stone to talk the language of the African primitives, but can these people, with their lives full of cars and telephones and electric shavers, make us doubt for an instant the genius of the artists whom they imitate parrot-like, copying enthusiastically the intonation but not the sense of their art?

Of course, from time to time I come across puppet shows given by old women whose foolishness is so charming, or by intellectual snobs who are so cultivated, that I wonder for a moment whether, impotent and useless, this art really does deserve attention. But the mood of doubt is short-lived. Can one hold it against the puppet theatre that in it, as in all the other arts, there are a few people who have come to it by accident or who quite simply have no talent? Of course not. It has every right to the place it occupies among the arts of spectacle. Its impact upon the public can be very profound and is not yet being used to the full.

A good half-century has passed since I first started giving puppet shows; for over thirty years I have been director of the State Central Puppet Theatre, Moscow, and the feeling that I am only just beginning to understand the greatness of this art has never left me. I have put on more than fifty plays in this theatre, and never have I lost the feeling that these are only the first steps towards the play of which I shall be able to say: "At last...!"

What ought it to be like, this play of my dreams?

In the first place it must be necessary, really necessary, to men. A great many men. Not to a dozen intellectual snobs, not to a hundred connoisseurs, not to a thousand theatre-lovers, but to tens of thousands of Soviet citizens. The première of such a play must be a real event, not just for the theatre but for the whole of society, as was the production of *Tartuffe* by Molière's company, as was the première of *The Cherry Orchard* at the Moscow Art Theatre. As were, in the case of films, *The Battleship 'Potemkin'*, *Chapaev*, *La Fièvre de l'Or*, *Rome–11 o'clock*. As once were the plays about the Russian popular hero Petroushka or the French hero Guignol. But for a puppet play to be an event of real social importance it must be an organic expression of an idea that springs from life itself, from the present day. The public must always feel that this play could only be put on as a puppet play. And this feeling can only exist when the subject and the particular qualities of the characters demand, really demand, the use of puppets to present them to the public.

What is it, then, that an inanimate puppet can express

and a flesh-and-blood actor cannot? What is its power? Strange as it may seem, its power lies in the very fact that it is inanimate. If an actor on a stage sits down in an armchair and hitches up his trouser legs so that his knees do not spoil the crease, the audience may well not notice it. But if the same movement is made by a puppet, the audience is likely to burst into applause because the puppet has made fun of all the men who make this movement.

On the stage, a man may portray another man but he cannot portray man in general because he is himself a man. The puppet is not a man and for that very reason it can give a living portrayal of man in general.

A young girl may be very beautiful; but it is only *her* beauty and *her* youth. The young girl created by a Praxiteles or a Konenkov is beautiful too, but her beauty no longer belongs to her; it represents the beauty and the youth of thousands of living girls, and this is precisely because this young girl is herself inanimate.

The puppet is a plastic generalization of a living being: man, reindeer, dove. The puppet is a sculpture; in animating this sculpture the puppeteer creates a dynamic generalization of a living being; man, reindeer, or dove. The process by which the inanimate becomes animate seems to the audience to be a real miracle. And this applies to all ages; children and adults react alike.

This miracle is what makes the art of puppetry different from the plastic arts, which are static, and at the same time places it in the category of the spectacle, of dynamic art. The same miracle makes the puppet theatre different from any spectacle in which man actually appears, that is to say, any kind of 'human' theatre, which does indeed involve a remodelling of personality–the actor playing a character other than himself–but not this process by which the inanimate takes life, not this change into an entirely different kind of being.

When the puppet finds itself in the hands of a real actor, one who believes deeply in the reality of what he is presenting to the public, who is profoundly moved by the miracle I have described, the impression made, the emotions aroused by the puppet can be extremely strong. Surprise, delight, laughter, anguish, and breathless excitement are all there.

I am not the only person to have known the incomparable happiness, measurable in seconds, in minutes, and even in tens of minutes, of seeing the miracle of a puppet suddenly being brought to life in the hands of a true artist.

I cannot forget seeing Petroushka, with his wooden head, his enormous nose and his painted eyes, stupid, naïve, sly, irascible Petroushka. Behind the screen stood that last representative of the popular Russian fairground puppet theatre–Ivan Afinogenovich Zaitsev. He was old and grey-haired. He held in his mouth, pressed against his palate, a little silver "pichtchik", a sort of whistle which emitted shrill squeaking sounds. Petroushka shouted in this piercing and inhuman voice and dealt mighty blows right and left with his stick. He was a living being of flesh and blood; he had a heart and a soul, a mind and a personality. Yet he was at the same time a miserable rag above which bobbed a painted wooden head, carved with knife and chisel by Zaitsev himself. It was the miracle of Galatea over again, but this Pygmalion, old Zaitsev, had not been struck by the fact that his creation had become a living being; he had simply been filled with joy by it, and he had passed his joy on to all of us. To all those who saw with their own eyes Zaitsev's Petroushka. To all of them—children and grown men.

I am not the only one to have been happy watching Špejbl and Hurvínek, lovingly created by the Czech Josef Skupa. When we read a fine book the characters in it penetrate our life just as though they were real people, they become our friends, our enemies, our close acquaintances; we give them our love. In just the same way these two characters, not out of the pages of a book but from a puppet theatre, came into my life. And not only into mine, but into the lives of many thousands of children and adults, in Prague, in Bratislava, in Brno and Olomouc. Into the lives of all those–Russians, Poles, Hungarians, Bulgarians, Rumanians, Frenchmen—who met even once these two marvellous beings, Špejbl and Hurvínek, who saw their wooden bodies, carved by Gustav Nossek, and understood their vibrant souls, created by Josef Skupa.

The play *The Night before Christmas*, after Gogol, disappeared long ago from the playbills of the Central Puppet Theatre, nevertheless I often recall it. I had a great friend in that play, and I cannot forget him because one can never forget a real friend. It was a very simple puppet, made from a scrap of material, which danced on three of the puppet-master's fingers. It was Gogol's Devil. He was waiting for his lady, Solocha, and warming himself at the stove. The stove burned his back, but after the terrible frost of that Christmas Eve it was just what he needed. Then Solocha poured him a drink of vodka. He lapped it from the glass like a puppy. Once drunk, he began to sing.

Semion Samodur brought this devil to life, thus presenting the audience with a marvellous friend, now man, now puppy, now monkey. A good-for-nothing and a good companion at the same time; now fit only to be kicked out of doors, now the best of men.

We have not revived Gozzi's *The Reindeer King* at the Theatre for many years, but Truffaldino, that rather foolish philosopher, always in love and always deceived, brought to life by Yevgeniy Speranskiy, is one of my best friends.

In Isidor Stok's *Divine Comedy* a living god moulds a man out of clay and sets it on the grass. It is an inanimate puppet, dead. The god breathes life into his man and departs. From the wings there appears the 'soul'—the puppet-master Zinovii Gherdt. He approaches the puppet, this inanimate Adam, and Adam comes alive. There are two miracles here: the miracle of the god creating the man and the miracle of the puppet-master who gives life to inert matter. The god's miracle is a doubtful one—it is not a real miracle and that is why the audience laughs at it. The puppet-master's miracle is a real one and the audience applauds.

In the hands of the puppet-master the puppet is all-powerful, if both puppet and puppet-master are good and if there is an aim which justifies giving a living soul to the puppet. When it is done solely for the sake of animating an inanimate object, the puppet-master's miracle disappears, becomes nothing more than an illusionist's trick. Lacking any lasting spiritual reality, it arouses no emotion in us and we are merely curious to know 'how it's done'. A puppet coming alive is not just a trick, it is a character being born. And if we know that these characters must not imitate man—that is, that they must not be a model of the human body and the human mind but must condense, synthesize, all that is essential and characteristic in the various features of human nature—then we understand why from the collision of these characteristics something is created with a new and wider meaning to which our hearts respond with deep emotion.

Puppets can debunk mercilessly; by simply making us laugh they can make us loathe the object of their attacks. Puppets are at home in all types of comedy—from farce to the most acid satire, even to the lampoon, a weapon which they have used more than once in the course of their history.

Puppets can be beautiful, as any sculpture can be, universalizing and giving expression to the very idea of beauty. The puppet can be gentle and appealing as a kitten, graceful as a snake, swift as a falcon; it generalizes and expresses the essence of every sentiment. Romantic, heroic, tragic—puppets can be all of these. That is why in the old mysteries the gods were represented by puppets. Puppets were the first to present the legend of Doctor Faust who sold his soul to the Devil. In this popular version for puppets, there is an amazing pair of characters: the tragic character of the alchemist, and the comic character of his servant. The Devil tricks Faust, but is tricked in turn by Pickle Herring, the servant. Pickle Herring is more intelligent, more practical, and more resourceful than his master. He is the people. The puppet is not a man, it is an allegory of man. Like all allegories, it has the power of generalizing reality. In the constant struggle of artists to understand life, to grasp it, allegory always has been and always will be an important weapon. But that is not all. It is with the help of this very process known as allegory that artists have often pinpointed the most burning topical problems. The legends and tales of all peoples and lands have always been topical at the time of their formation, and it is for this very reason that folk memory preserves them so carefully in language by making something akin to common nouns out of the names of the heroes of these tales, these heroes who personify human wickedness, greed, stupidity, courage, wisdom, and goodness.

The message that Aesop passed to La Fontaine, La Fontaine to Krylov, and Krylov to the fable-writers of the present day is enlivened by an amazing up-to-dateness. Need I mention the tales of Saltykov-Stchedrin, with their burning topicality? And Swift's satirical novel? And Mayakovsky? All his work, or almost all of it, bears the stamp of allegory. And I think it is true to say that the legend of Doctor Faust itself is at once tragedy and fable.

Do I then want to put on a popular-style *Faust*? No. Do I want to put on in all their splendour the heroic medieval spectacles of the Sicilian puppets? No.

My dream is to see in the puppet theatre works as rich and as full of passionate conviction as those I have mentioned, but which deal with topical issues, which are modern in their form and in their ideas.

I am waiting for the Swift, the Saltykov-Stchedrin, the Mayakovsky of our time to present their works in puppet plays. I do not know what their names will be; it is possible that they exist already, that I even know them already. Perhaps one of them is writing even now a really revolutionary play dominated by the same human pathos, by the same satirical and allegorical vision that characterize Mayakovsky's famous *Mystery Bouffe*.

I have seen many interesting things in puppet plays shown at home and abroad. I have seen interesting puppets and remarkable puppet-masters. I have admired the wonderful imagination of producers and designers; but I have never seen a production that was a unity, a monolith, purely and specifically a puppet play, burningly topical, necessary, moving, an event of real social importance. I dream of seeing one. And of taking part in its creation. For I am a producer, I work in this art and I have many friends, artists who share the same idea, all gathered together by our theatre: our playwrights, our producers, our puppet-masters, our designers, our composers. So why should I not cherish this dream?

Actor and Puppeteer

by Harro Siegel

German (Federal Republic). An artist, who taught for many years at the Brunswick College of Visual Arts, and whose theatre has visited England. Harro Siegel has never been interested in the commercial possibilities of the puppet theatre, but has developed the art of the marionette to a most exquisite degree.

In this article we shall try to deal not with theories and speculations but with facts and actual experience. It is self-evident that no one can be a puppeteer without also being an actor. In both cases we find, behind the play-acting, man as a mover, as an actor. The difference lies only in the instrumentation of his means of expression. The actor's instrument is his own body, his face, his voice; that of the puppeteer is his puppet. He acts through the puppet, he moves the puppet (indirectly if it is a marionette or a rod puppet, directly if it is a glove puppet), he hides behind it, he serves it. Hence the direct vital impact of the glove puppet, hence also the dreamlike, floating, submissive quality of the marionette, with finally the rod puppet appearing to share in both realms.

If we regard these puppets, these representations of human and other beings, as a kind of mask of the whole body, a mask which the operator is not wearing but holding more or less away from himself, we touch on one of those points where stage acting and puppetry blend into each other. I do not know whether historians have proved it, or whether it can be proved—but I cannot visualize any theatre having its origin in anything other than the play of masks, whether we are thinking of ritual dances in pre-history or among 'primitives' or of Greek and Roman antiquity, or of the theatre of East Asia.

Let us remember also that theatre is based on the transformation of reality—i. e., on art—that even a realistic representation can give us pleasure or move us only if it appears as "perfect art, as second nature—but not when everybody believes that he need only display his own naked character to offer something that is worthy of applause" (Goethe). For many centuries the human theatre knew only male performers, with female parts being acted by men. It is interesting therefore to recall that Goethe commended this practice because "in such a performance the concept of imitation, the thought of art, remains ever alive" and "a kind of conscious illusion is produced by skilful acting". The result is "doubly charming in that the actors are not women but represent women". The actor therefore plays "not himself, but a third and essentially strange character. This character we come to know the better because it has been observed and thought out; what we see is not the thing itself, but the result of the thing"—and therein, in Goethe's view, lies the ultimate essence of all art. We might add Schiller's remark that "illusion should never reach reality, for where nature prevails there art must flee".

One should not therefore stipulate dogmatically that in puppetry only the puppet should be visible and never its human operator. Just because we have lately seen the most varied forms of interplay between puppets and human actors—admittedly there have been excesses and fashionable mistakes—we should hold on to that idea of transformed reality as a yardstick. Provided both puppet and operator serve this higher entity, provided they remain, as it were, on a common plane, they will not only open up fertile virgin ground for the theatre but also reclaim a timeless 'theatre-in-itself'. It is in this light, I believe, that we must view such varied phenomena as the operator appearing in full view with his glove puppet (Obraztsov) or marionette (Roser), or the play of hands alone (Yves Joly, Kovacz, Mensching), the 'black theatre' of the Czechs, and the interplay, developed so impressively in Poland, between live actors, masked and unmasked, and rod, glove, or string puppets (Guignol, Zwyrtala, Pastoralka). For this reason it is perfectly legitimate for puppet groups to turn to masks and for masked shows to be included in puppetry festivals. Hence also the mutual recognition between mime (Marceau) and puppeteer.

A wealth of cross-fertilization—and why not? The Japanese Nô gave its elements to the Bunraku, and the Kabuki actors in turn took Bunraku as their model. This kind of thing may well be possible in our own countries today. Gordon Craig's dream of the "actor as super-marionette" means just that transformation, and it is in this transformation that puppetry and theatre meet. Craig did not discover his reforming ideas in East Asia, but he found them confirmed there as a basic truth of the theatre. Bertolt Brecht, too, had already gone far in developing his style when, enchanted by the Chinese theatre and its male actors of female parts, he wrote his essay about "alienation effects in Chinese dramatic art".

Encounters on an almost world-wide scale between puppet theatres from many countries have been made possible by the efforts of UNIMA intended to promote neither mannered imitations nor a hotch-potch of untranslatable stage styles, but cross-fertilization within the theatrical framework. We observe with increasing clarity the decisive influence that has been exerted on stage design, both in the human and the puppet theatre, by contemporary painting. We are instinctively reminded of the religious art and the carved wooden altars of the late Middle Ages when the arts and the theatre were alive in the same medium and when the public re-encountered its mystery plays in painting and sculpture.

We might point here to the excellent investigations of Krystyna Mazur, who has traced the to-and-fro of similar developments in our own time in the Polish theatre and puppet play—a very salutary reflection about the supranational exchanges between theatre, masks, puppetry, and the visual arts, with many a good point on such questions as: tradition or modernity, rule and method or imagination and experiment, safety or risk. Its meaning for us is that the puppet theatre, regardless of its individuality, is not (or should not be) an isolated artistic phenomenon. Instead, we puppeteers should place our special knowledge into the framework of a higher unity and not be afraid of forays into the uncharted no-man's-land of new forms of utterance; we should view stylistic boundaries not only as something that separates but also as something that is permeable to ideas, something that encourages us to draw together more closely, something that unites us. In this way our art will attract enthusiastic young people seeking their own fulfilment; in this way puppetry as a children's theatre will, with its best achievements, attract also an adult audience. One need only recall the successes of Wilkowski and Kilian in *Zwyrtala the Musician*.

What is intended, however, is not a blurring of boundaries, not a 'marionettization' of the human theatre, let alone a puppet performance as a miniature imitation of the human theatre. What we mean is an intensification, a concentration, a heightening and a deepening, of both within their common framework of rules.

I cannot discuss the interplay between actor and puppeteer without a few observations about Bunraku–first because it represents one of the most precious and artistically most perfect forms of puppetry, whose survival into our time must be regarded as a great piece of fortune, and secondly because in it is shown the subordination of the actor to the "total work of art" in purer form than anywhere else. Finally, Bunraku is just as much stylistically pure puppetry as it is theatre-in-itself; it has taken over a lot from the human theatre and handed on to it even more.

In Bunraku the operators are in full view together with the puppets; each of the principal puppets is manipulated by three operators. The main operator wears his professional clothes, a kimono with fanned-out wing-like shoulder pieces. The other two operators, by way of contrast, are swathed in black. It is surprising and wonderful to see the accomplished co-ordination with which these three operate their puppet as though directed by one single will, as if they were subordinating themselves to their puppet, serving it, following it as passive yielders with the puppet as the active agent. Even more astonishing is the fact that neither do the operators speak themselves nor do the puppets receive their voice from an invisible speaker; instead, in full view at the side of the stage, a kneeling reciter reads all dialogues, stage directions,

and linking narrations. The puppet operators, on the one hand, are so entirely absorbed in handling their puppets that their faces have an inward look, an utterly drained appearance, yet the speaker, on the other hand, is so profoundly engaged in his text that often one cannot tear one's eyes away from him. He throws himself into his text with complete abandon, in a kind of semi-chant totally unlike everyday speech. He is accompanied by the lute-player who seems to be one with him. We thus have five men engaged in giving a semblance of life to one single puppet–and all of them in full view. We are witnessing here the birth and development of scenic art: theatrical theatre, alienation *par excellence*, a sense of high purpose transcending cause and effect. Tradition and practice have so completely perfected this pattern of movement and expression that positively nothing earthly is left clinging to it.

In all three types of the ancient Japanese theatre–Nô, Bunraku, and Kabuki–we are witnessing a transformation, an exchange of realities, as though peering over a painter's shoulder. The lines, dots, and areas placed on the canvas by the brush in the artist's hand, the outline and colour–all these produce before our eyes something new, the 'artefact' embodying the natural substances, the picture. Similarly, in the theatre (directly with the actor, indirectly with the puppeteer) mask, movement, colour, and shape under the lights, words, and sounds transform themselves in front of us into a new combination, a metamorphosis. It is vitally important that in the world of today there should still be such a mysterious theatrical form as the Bunraku. One notices that it "was established in the garden of mysteries, by the flank of the temple" (Alastair). One must hope that it will live on–for all of us.

This apparent digression was intended as an eye-opener and to establish standards of comparison. Puppetry seeking merely verisimilitude and realism belongs to the sphere of sideshows and waxworks. But the true puppet theatre, the stage of illusive humans and illusive beings, the theatre of "symbols and figures", is closely concerned with the general developments. It does not accompany them as a marginal gloss but reflects them, as it were, in distilled form. The foundation of the first UNIMA (Union Internationale des Marionnettes) between the two wars and the foundation of the second in 1957, together with the world-wide encounters which have taken place in consequence, have increasingly clarified our ideas of the role of puppetry as an essential theatre of "form" or of "conscious illusion" or of "alienation".

The contributions to this book are intended to illuminate a few aspects and vital questions of the life and growth of puppetry in our century. UNIMA is not an organization set up for itself. It is a vessel, an instrument, a platform, a helpmate –aiming, on the one hand, at rousing and keeping awake the artistic spirit and the pleasure of using movable puppets as parables of life, and, on the other, at collecting and reflecting these efforts, growing pains, and joys like a mirror. All true artistic achievement springs from the depths of the soul. It cannot be manufactured, proclaimed, or propagated. Perhaps it will be said one day that the puppet stage of the first half of our century–a period of great transitions–has now and then, between tradition and experiment, between East and West, between success and failure, illuminated something of the image of man, some measure of true humanism. Puppetry is like a magic key, a secret writing, a flute awaiting its legitimate player, its Shakespeare, its Chikamatsu–its poet.

Where have we come from? Where are we going?

by Jean-Loup Temporal

French. A practical puppeteer with a marked philosophy of the art of puppetry.

Born of magic and mysticism, our art and our profession certainly pre-date the birth of the theatre. Their survival and their continued development in this century of scientific culture prove that they are vital, strong, necessary, even immortal. Histories of the puppet tell us about its past, and international meetings testify to its revival in the present, but what can we predict for its future?

Much . . . Let us leave aside new 'markets'–such as television, which will be calling more and more upon the puppet; and teaching, which will make ever greater use of the powers of persuasion of the doll; and medicine, which will exploit its hypnotic power–and let us try to look at the problem from another angle: that of puppetry as a dramatic art. Will the puppet interest adults as it has done in the past–or children as it does today? The question is of secondary importance and depends only on a psycho-ontological adaptation of repertoire and technique.

The problem of the future of the puppet theatre lies not there but rather in the form of expression it must discover and formulate in order to break out of its past, its routines, its traditions, its myths, and to adapt itself to the public of today and of tomorrow. Without losing sight of the principles it has acquired over the centuries, it must find a new ethos to suit our times. For this it will no longer be enough for it to find its laws within itself; it will have to turn to other forms of expression: the cinema, the theatre, dancing; to other kinds of spectacle: sporting events, competitions, circuses, shows;

to other arts: painting, sculpture, music; adapting itself all the time to new techniques and closely following scientific research. In fact, our art must become again a great popular theatre, a theatre of participation, a theatre of animation, a theatre of research; but it must find once more a sense of social purpose! What is it today?

Watched over by a technological and highly planned society, we no longer have to fight. With his safety, his welfare assured, man is losing his taste for danger; we must at least preserve his taste for entertainment. Here the puppet has a lot to offer–perhaps more than the theatre: it can play 'for the audience', but at the same time 'with' it, making it feel it is something more than just a crowd.

Fifty years ago it was amateurs who were responsible for the revival of puppetry, and the result today is some remarkable little masterpieces of plastic art in motion or some excellent little didactic pieces. But all these seem to lead to a dead end because so often they lack the elements which constitute the very basis of the dramatic arts: inner communion with the audience. An audience wants to be concerned, gripped, uplifted; what they believe is more important than what they see. So we need to establish a dramatic literature for the contemporary puppet theatre. There lies the whole problem; that is all there is to it.

The question is being asked throughout the world, in the same way, with the same force. Technical problems are of secondary importance, so are aesthetic ones, so are financial ones. Everyone who goes regularly to international meetings recognizes that the problem of the 'dramaturgy' is there and that each is trying to resolve it as well as he can.

This is the hardest problem of our research, for in order to adapt to the modern world it is no longer possible to turn to philosophy, mysticism, or aesthetics; instead we must create a new synthesis of them, and find new power, starting from the forceful psychological effect of the doll, or the object, in movement and conflict. With enthusiasm and perseverance we are all seeking a solution to this vital problem. With each of us lighting a bit of the way, I see no reason why we should not eventually find our road to Damascus.

The Eternal Conflict

by Henryk Jurkowski

Polish. The head of the government department in the Ministry of Culture that is concerned with puppet theatres. The Polish puppet theatres are some of the most original and most brilliant in Europe.

There have been many different stages in the history of the puppet theatre. It has passed through the hands of rogues and charlatans; it has been in the service of priests and politicians. Today we see it as an artistic theatre. The immediate beginnings of our puppetry must be sought at the turn of the century when a revolt against naturalism induced artists and theatrical reformers to turn their attention to the puppet stage. Gordon Craig, with typical overstatement, says in *Puppets and Poets*, "The puppet is the actor's primer"–an observation made with an eye to the requirements of the theatre. And Sokoloff, in his *Thoughts on My Theatre of Musical Dynamism*, rightly reverts to the old mystical conception of the puppet theatre: "Out of an urge for the artistic freedom of his creative will man invented puppetry. By this invention man freed himself from his belief in an inescapable fate; he created a world of figures determined by himself and thus consolidated his will, his logic, and his aesthetic–in short, he became a little god ruling his own world."

The charm of the puppet theatre lies in the great range of possibilities open to the will of the creative artist, subject, of course, to the 'material'. That, in my opinion, is the reason why artists concern themselves with the puppet theatre and why puppets are used in stage productions–by Reinhardt, for instance, and in certain Bauhaus productions. But this is a subjective aspect of the problem–"from the point of view of the artist".

What then does the puppet theatre mean to the public and what did it mean to them in the past? In antiquity it was a ritual and an entertainment. In the Middle Ages it represented the magic reality of hobgoblins who came to life in the hands of itinerant puppeteers who were often ventriloquists as well. Later it became a religious performance and miracle play, later still dramatic theatre in miniature, and a puppet theatre with its own autonomous life. Finally, it became a theatre for children, with the adult audience drifting away from it to more attractive genres.

In his speech at the UNIMA Congress in Bucharest in 1958 Sergei Obraztsov equated the puppet's social artistic value with its 'synthesizing' characteristics—its ability to represent the universal and the typical. This point of view successfully combines both the subjective and the objective aspects of the problem. It touches upon the final result of the artist's work.

For anyone wanting to create "a world dependent only on himself" the material of the puppet and the characteristics arising from it provide the main element. Such characteristics, for instance, are facial features and the proportions of the figures, which are easily shaped. Such, also, are the lead-filled feet which determine the character of its movements. Tin, cloth, wood, plastic, willow-cane—every one of these materials has its own peculiarities, and that is why Craig, in *Puppets and Poets*, has rightly remarked: "I mean you don't move it, you let it move itself; that's the art."

Explanations about the material or the independent character of the puppet were just as frequent as efforts to convince the audience that it was looking at living though miniaturized actors. The mime of antiquity and the Middle Ages, in spite of his ventriloquist's skill, remained to his audience a simple mountebank who entertained them by means of puppets. The element of entertainment predominated over that of imitation, as shown in some cases by the fact that the mime would readily transform himself into a storyteller in front of his puppet stage.

On other occasions the puppets had to play the part of well-disguised dwarfs. It was difficult to believe that Brioché,

accused of witchcraft in Switzerland, was entirely innocent, when even Martin Powell fixed a net across the front of his stage as late as the eighteenth century in order to hide the strings of his marionettes from the eyes of the audience. There was clearly something in the atmosphere of the period which made illusionist tricks so popular. The practice must have been very widespread if Samuel Foote, as we know, opposed it so vigorously in demanding "the original art of puppetry".

Imitation of humans is encountered to this day in many theatres, and lately the technique of the 'black theatre' has also been brought into its service. Powell's net is replaced here by muslin, which hides no longer the strings of the marionettes but the actors operating in the dark, beyond the skilfully handled spotlights. The analogy with the net, however, is very obvious. The illusion of life is thus created by concealing the secret of the puppet's movement.

A different case is that of deliberate artistic illusion. This knowledge can result from a marked stylization of the puppet and its action or from the fact that the process of animation of the puppet takes place before the spectator's eyes. The former instance represents an entirely new phenomenon, unknown in the past as far as I am aware—excepting the glove puppet and the shadow puppet which stand outside the art of puppetry; nowadays the principle of stylization has prevailed almost universally. Animation of the puppet in front of the spectator's eyes goes back to the tradition of the mime, a tradition still preserved in cabaret and variety shows. This trend reached its peak under Obraztsov and Roser and is related, in the theatrical field, to the "stage upon the stage".

Among puppeteers Samuel Foote was the first to champion this principle deliberately and emphatically in order to destroy the scenic illusion. It was he who, in "The Primitive Puppet Show" in 1773, introduced a gendarme on the stage, acted by a human, who tried to arrest the puppet. In *Tragedy à la Mode* he made use of large, possibly flat, marionettes whose words were spoken by a live actor standing in their midst. Today this principle is as popular as the poetic stylization of the puppet. In this sense, therefore, the anti-imitation trends have proved victorious in the present-day theatre.

They are reflected in the Rumanian "Tandarica" Theatre and in the Polish "Lalka", just as in the endeavours of the French puppeteers or in the manner in which the Hungarians are using their traditional folk art.

"Tandarica" reveals its artistic programme both in the transgression of the bounds of probability and in parody (very brilliantly in *Hand with Five Fingers*), and it is equally reflected in the sublimation of the subject by way of philosophical rhetoric and emphatic emotionalism as in *The Little Prince* by Saint-Exupéry. "Lalka" introduces the principle of the "stage upon the stage" (in *The Troubles of Guignol*) and points to the origin of the puppet–Zwyrtala, a mountain peasant figure drawn on glass, and Pierrot the tiger, a film character now moving in a three-dimensional world. In the theatre of masks, represented by the "Groteska" Theatre in Cracow, this principle has resulted in one and the same figure appearing in two versions–with and without mask.

Yves Joly extends the scope of the puppet theatre by the creative movements of his hands and fingers, and the Hungarians are doing the same by a burlesque man-against-man show raised to the level of theatrical convention. In this way our contemporary puppet theatre is in a position to enrich the stage with values hitherto unknown or at best dreamed of only by theatrical reformers. The thematic and uniform character of a material lacking all biological elements ensures the harmony and homogeneity of the picture in a way unknown on the live stage. At the same time the anti-imitation trends are bringing the public into contact with the creative process on the stage and are showing it the multiple meaning of this process in its own language. But the most important thing is that these aspects originate from the natural peculiarities of the puppet itself: "Let it move itself".

The Puppet as a Poetic Symbol

by Stefan Lenkisch

Rumanian. One of the producers of the "Tandarica" Theatre, Bucharest; author of several studies of contemporary puppet art.

The explosive emergence of new techniques, the extension of its frontiers, and the discovery of more far-reaching possibilities than have been handed down to us by tradition–these are the valuable gains made by the art of puppetry in our age.

This explosion is no mirage; it is not a merely superficial event, but one that has transformed all artistic concepts in the field of puppetry. The past twenty years represent a true period of rebirth; the number of permanent theatres is growing at a staggering rate, original companies and powerful artistic personalities are making their appearance. A form of dramatic production has come into being which not only takes account of the achievements of the theatrical stage but which in its turn affects the development of the live theatre. As soon as striking artistic means came to be used for the creation of dramatic subjects–means specific to and in character with the puppet stage–public interest began to grow and a new attitude began to develop towards the puppet theatre. At one time merely a 'curiosity', a 'skilled craft', the puppet theatre has today become a poetic form of art on a high plane. The attempt to unravel the meaning of the puppet anew in each performance produced an increasingly well-defined and, at the same time, increasingly comprehensive aesthetic of this art form. Here lies the main problem for the future. It may even embrace all past problems of the turbulent history of puppetry.

This history is not only the history of our theatre but also that of every single member of our puppet company, including my own history as a producer. To begin with, we demanded no more of our puppet interpreters than that they should be original actors. The fascination of the puppet, moving in the same way as its human giant model, lies in its appealing awkwardness and has all the charm of such awkwardness. Whether creators or spectators, we all gazed on our puppets like men enchanted, in much the same way as we would gaze spellbound on a mechanical ballet or a musical box.

That was in the beginning. Soon we began to realize an important fact: if our puppet performed one particular movement to perfection the spectator would gain the impression that it could perform any conceivable movement. However, so long as the puppet theatre depends on the action of the operator it stays put at the stage of the imitative theatre, since it is adapted to the specific detail of the human type. No doubt this leads to a certain perfection and clearly also satisfies the audience by filling them with amazement at the unusual character of the performers. But this amazement is not a genuine artistic experience: it is not aimed at revealing in full the hidden human significance of what is happening on the stage. Moreover, there were a lot of things which were not compatible with such 'perfection'—indeed, they even ran counter to it. The more eloquent the character of the puppet, the more indifferent it was to the spoken text, the more eloquent very often was its silence, more eloquent than whole pages of lyrical or humorous text.

We had to make a fresh start. We tried to find a clear answer to the question: What is the puppet? We contrasted the fairground puppet, bursting with vitality, with the dazzling modern puppet. We tried to get a clear idea about those "few minutes of real art" in every performance. We extended the range of genres by staging heroic poems, farces, political satire, and tragic epics; we resorted to the grotesque show, the pantomime, the variety show; we made our puppets sing, dance, and remain silent. We asked ourselves: How must a puppet act, how must it speak, what artistic value has a shock produced by tricks? Needless to say, these questions were not considered *en masse*, or in the course of some discussion or conference; they confronted us during long hours of work, in the course of dozens of performances. We watched the serious, expressive countenance of the puppet and we tried to wrest from it the secret of its character and significance.

Now and again the metaphor, the poetic symbols, are produced with fascinating simplicity: the movement of a rope in *The Little Princess* conjures up the unforgettable image of a snake. But in order to present the long and thorny Odyssey of the fairy princess we had to resort to a multitude of colours and sounds, light and shade. These were supplied for us by the painter who gave new form to the full depth and delicate nuances of the anguish of the princess searching for her husband.

In *Hand with Five Fingers* a night-club brawl starts with an explosion of bottles, glasses, and plates; it continues in a mêlée of fighting bodies, kicking legs, and finally crashing chairs. This satirical sequence is a metaphor, a poetic symbol of the endless fights in film thrillers. The scenic picture is many-faceted, but integrated and concentrated, full of comical fancy such as can only be encompassed and represented by the imagination of the puppet.

In the limitlessly vast expanse of snow there appear the imprints of a penguin's feet, without the hero himself being seen. This simple overwhelming symbol for Apollodorus' lonely journey across a cold and desert Alaska radiates boundless sadness. Even as a puppet an elephant would hardly seem to command a very rich scale of emotional expressions. Yet the inquisitive little elephant in Kipling's story combines these so economically that its naïve yet rich world is abundantly suggested.

The break with sentimentality (we might say, the "alienation effect"), this witty, ironical self-deprecation which manifests itself in a kind of provocative shock, in a surprise solution invariably in puppet terms—are these perhaps the secret of the puppet, of its ever-present ability to create poetic symbols? I believe that that is so.

The fact that in our choice and use of the means of expression we must apply, on the one hand, a strict precision of movement and, on the other, an abundance of fantasy is undoubtedly one of the secrets of the puppet's triumph as an exponent of poetic symbolism. I believe that it owes its triumphs to the fact that the part, the character, it acts is an interlacing of many elements with the spoken text: the plastic realization of the puppet, its movement and the scenic picture, the lighting and the music all contributing their share. All these give rise to a living entity—the hero.

I believe that the essential is contained in that synthesis. It is in this way that the part, the acting character, is born and that the dramatic idea crystallizes. Shape and meaning of the scenic plot derive from the same synthesis. The interplay of proportions and the harmony—*i. e.*, the balance—of these elements determine the feelings and ideas that the play triggers off in the audience. The illusion is the stronger and the puppet's power of expression the deeper, the closer and more integrated this connection is. This, in my view, is the road that leads us to the poetic symbol.

In the live theatre the author, the stage director, or the producer can occasionally cover up some shortcoming or other by various effects or tricks, or by the charm of an actor; in the puppet theatre this is not possible. The frank silence with which the puppet faces us every time when we have gone astray is at times shattering. No trick can help us here, no trick can make up for the artistic truth the puppet demands.

It is as well that this should be so. For thus we are compelled to seek for great art in the puppet theatre and to concentrate on man, on his high striving, on his poetic view of the world.

That is the heavy gate through which lies the road to his future, to poetry.

Tradition and Experiment

by George Speaight

English. Both a practical performer and a scholar, author of the standard history of puppets in England.

The puppet theatre is an ancient art with great traditions; it is also, in many countries, a young art with great scope for experiment. Can these two elements be combined in a synthesis that has value for the puppeteer of today?

In the countries of Western Europe where the puppet has a long and honoured history, three main strands of development may be distinguished. First, there is the theatre of folk tale. The wandering puppet showman played an important role as a popularizer of traditional stories; he helped to spread a native folk literature. His themes were the same as those of ballad singers and the printers of chapbooks. Secondly, there is the theatre of wonder. As the technique of the marionette developed, audiences were attracted by the remarkable feats it could display. Invisible methods of control were perfected; skeletons fell to pieces and reassembled themselves; Harlequin flew round the auditorium; the old lady climbed a balloon and floated up into the clouds. Thirdly, there is the theatre of satire. Italian opera was parodied; public personalities, fads of fashion, and political programmes were made the butt of the puppet's gentle ridicule. The puppet show became an animated caricature.

What function have these aspects of the puppet theatre in modern society? We cannot, nor should we wish to, merely repeat the past. The puppet theatre must speak in a new society with new accents. But I believe that the traditions of the past provide foundations upon which we can and should build. Let us consider the adaptation of these three strands in the world today.

The peasant society to which the theatre of folk tale played for so many centuries barely exists today. But just as the folk tale itself has now become the literature of children, so the puppet theatre is now widely regarded as the theatre of children. Some puppeteers resent this as they wish to practise an adult art. We may all agree that the puppet theatre is not *only* for children, and any puppeteer is at liberty not to play for children at all. But children provide the freshest, most responsive audience for whom any artist can play; the necessity of playing for children is not a cramping restriction but a liberation from the conventional confines of adult entertainment. This is our golden opportunity. But the puppeteer must *want* to play for children. I am afraid that there are too many puppeteers who play for children reluctantly, because that is where the audience lies. One too often hears the phrase, "this is only for children". Such an attitude is a betrayal of our trust.

The theatre of wonder has, indeed, lost most of its wonder today. Its tricks are performed far more efficiently on film and television. Conjuring tricks with puppets possess the attraction of any technical expertise, but they lead up a blind alley. There is little future here. But there is one element in this genre that has an abiding appeal. The trick figures of other days belonged to a world apart: the dissectible skeleton, the three-headed Scaramouch, the expanding and contracting Cures, were all un-human characters, creatures of fantasy. In the world of fantasy the puppet remains the actor *par excellence* for those who have the imagination to follow him away from realism and naturalism.

Many modern puppeteers have shown themselves aware of the possibilities of the theatre of satire. The puppet is, indeed, an ideal vehicle for this type of entertainment. In order to flourish properly, however, it needs the right audience and the right surroundings. I would like to see a relaxed cabaret atmosphere for this kind of show, recapturing something of the ambience of the café society of nineteenth-century France or the coffee-house society of eighteenth-century England—in both of which the satirical puppet show flourished. The atmosphere of give-and-take between audience and actor is as important in this kind of show as it is in a children's theatre; I do not think it is often found.

The puppet theatre cannot live merely upon its traditions; in all the three strands of development that I have traced, the original type of presentation has no validity in the modern world—but by all means let us preserve something of these authentic traditions in museums and actual performances. Equally the puppeteer must experiment, to enlarge the scope of his art and to justify his claims as an artist. Yet all the three strands of most hopeful experiment are in fact developments of past tradition. The puppet theatre, whether presenting folk tale, fantasy, or satire, appeals to children—or to poets. It can appeal at the simplest level, or at the most sophisticated. And at whatever level it plays, it will succeed by imaginative experiment springing from ancient traditions.

The Vitality of a Tradition

by Maria Signorelli

Italian. A student of puppet history and the director of one of the few Italian puppet theatres with a modern approach to their art.

The vitality of a tradition cannot be seen in its unchanged acceptance, in its rigid imitation. Customs and artistic and intellectual trends change continually and give way to the new. Whatever dies or is destined to die never leaves a gap; it is invariably replaced by something new, something of the same kind, something akin to what preceded it. Anybody regretting the decline of various old customs and views should realize that his regrets spring from an inability to see the new that is for ever growing in the womb of the old.

However, the essential elements of national traditions–unless we wish to call them popular traditions straight away–are indestructible. Even when they adapt themselves to new trends, to new forms of expression which are widespread or even of international significance, their spirit does not die. It can be detected in certain nuances–indistinct, perhaps, but unmistakable.

Whatever losses in a tradition have to be replaced so that it can survive in a new form, this cannot be done by exorcism of the obsolete or the lost. Only through creative recollection does tradition become fertile, only if new life is breathed into its fundamental sensibility.

The rigid, almost ritual repetition of a series of actions, taking place amidst colours, notes, or barely discernible sounds which enchant the spectator–do these not, as do also many ballets for rod puppets, suggest to us a revival of the magic and religious style of our Sicilian puppet theatre? And are we not reminded also of the traditional popular glove puppets of Bologna, Naples, and Rome which we regard as the descendants of the Commedia dell'arte and which offer the same 'miracles' to their audiences as the sideshows of the sixteenth century?

The imaginative revival of that which is indestructible and human–that is the tradition represented by the puppet stage.

The Puppet Theatre: a Form of Visual or Dramatic Art?

by Erik Kolár

Czech. Dean of the Puppetry Department in the University of Prague–the only university in the world that offers a course, both practical and theoretical, in the puppet theatre.

In order to determine the specific character of the puppet theatre we must first of all find the *genus proximum* of which the puppet theatre is a special variant. At first sight this would seem to be quite simple. Even the name of our art form in the majority of languages suggests that it is a kind of theatre. Yet neither theory nor practice is entirely unambiguous in this respect. It is sometimes argued that the puppet theatre is, above all, a form of visual art. Those who hold this view believe that the puppet theatre expresses itself in the character of the puppet–*i.e.*, through an element of visual art. They moreover support their assertion by quoting the names of outstanding artists who have designed puppets or puppet stage décor. This and similar theories are found not only in Czechoslovakia (Otakar Zich, Karel Langer) where, especially in the twenties, the puppet theatre really was a domain of the visual arts. In a recent Polish book, *Polska plastyka teatralna*, Zenobiusz Strzelecki proves the importance of the visual element in the puppet theatre by referring to Klee, Léger, Picasso, Miró, and others who actively concerned themselves with this genre. From Strzelecki's essay one may conclude–though he does not say so explicitly–that he sees the puppet theatre as a kind of intermediate form between the theatre and the visual arts.

It is true, on the other hand, that the supporters of the theory that the puppet theatre is real theatre can outpoint their opponents by quoting such names as Craig, who wanted to drive the actor from the stage and replace him by a super-marionette, or Gaston Baty, who rated the puppet theatre higher than the live theatre. They can also quote Petr Bogatyrev, the Soviet ethnographer, who sees the puppet theatre as the very quintessence of the theatre, or Marcel Marceau, who establishes a kinship between the puppet theatre and the silent mime.

But neither the number of names nor their artistic weight can be the decisive argument. Instead we should ask which are the fundamental characteristics of theatrical art and which those of the visual arts, and having done so we should determine which of these are the preponderant characteristics of the puppet theatre.

Live Theatre	Puppet Theatre	Visual Art
a) is art in time and space		is art in space
b) represents the *development* of events and characters		represents the *state* of men or objects
c) exists only during actual performances		has lasting existence
d) is a product in which consumer witnesses the *creative process*		is a product in which consumer witnesses the *created product*
e) is an ever new reaction of actor or puppet operator to an ever new reaction of the audience, and hence variable from one performance to another		is fundamentally unchangeable
f) is always the work of a collective		is as a rule the work of an individual artist
g) is always and inevitably a synthetic work of art (composed of different art forms, such as literature, acting, direction, visual art, music, etc.) – *i.e.*, a universal work of art in the Wagnerian sense		the various kinds of visual art do not, as a rule, permeate each other
h) has as its basic characteristic: the actor	the puppet operator with his puppet as his instrument	a visual work of art expressed by shape, colour, and line

We might add that the decisive elements of the live theatre are the dramatic text, the actor, the scenic space, and a collective audience. They are the same elements as in the puppet theatre, except that here the actor is replaced by the puppet operator in inseparable unity with his puppet. The general basic laws of theatrical art apply also to the puppet theatre–in particular the law of action, the importance of conflict, the emotional effect combined with rational purpose, and the wealth of individual features of each character, expressed principally in the action but usually also through individualized speech.

From the above I deduce that puppetry belongs to the theatre.

Although I do not therefore view the puppet theatre as a form of visual art I do not, of course, deny that the part played in it by the visual artist is much more marked than it is in the big theatre (including opera, operetta, ballet, and pantomime). On the puppet stage, indeed, the dramatic figure is shaped not only through the human voice but also through what is in fact a piece of sculpture in action. Nevertheless, on the puppet stage as on the real stage the visual element is an ancillary factor subordinated to the producer's intentions and hence, in a sense, is a form of applied art.

A Producer's Reflections on the Roles of the Actor and the Designer

by Mikhail M. Korolov

Russian. Director of the Leningrad Bolshoi Puppet Theatre, one of Russia's leading puppet theatres and, in the opinion of some critics, superior to that of Moscow.

The art of puppetry is infinitely rich and varied, and even today we are far from having grasped all its possibilities. It is not surprising therefore that we puppeteers are passionately anxious to understand its intimate nature, the particular characteristics that make it what it is. There is every reason to believe that all the fundamental and inescapable characteristics of the puppet theatre—a theatre, an art in which the actor does not actually appear on the stage but makes use of an intermediary, an instrument, the puppet—will remain unchanged for as long as the puppet theatre continues to exist. In this essential quality lie all the secrets of our art.

Two vital and interdependent elements lie at the heart of the art of puppetry – the actor and the puppet. The existence of an actor necessarily implies that this is a dramatic form, because the actor must create characters, must play a part. From the professional point of view the actor must possess all the technical mastery that is required in the live theatre. But the puppet is a product of painting and of sculpture, a work of art created by the collaboration of a painter and a sculptor. This is why the puppet theatre is a hybrid born of the complex and organic fusion of two arts: the dramatic and the plastic. Only unity of action on the part of the artists working in these two fields can ensure uninterrupted development and a fine future for our theatre.

Of course, in many cases the balance is lost. Sometimes it is the plastic artist who is the more successful, sometimes it is the actor; this clearly cannot happen without leaving an unmistakable imprint upon the performance. But when this imbalance becomes deeper, more marked, the theatre is in mortal danger. I would quote as an example those plastic artists who, in their passion for innovation, create puppets which are perfectly flat, or motionless, or which bear no resemblance to any form that we are likely to meet with in real life–in short, meaningless abstractions. Admittedly, because they are so unusual, puppets of this kind can appear interesting, even beautiful; but what is there here for the actor? He must be reduced, it seems, to holding the puppet motionless in front of the audience or moving it to and fro, to being in fact a mere physical support for the work of the plastic artist. From here it is but a short step to mechanical puppets, moved by electricity. Then the puppet theatre would involve only one artist and would cease to be a puppet theatre.

To go to the other extreme, to neglect the contribution of the plastic artist, to refuse to acknowledge his claims, would be to turn the puppet theatre into a bad copy of the dramatic theatre; its actors would be powerful masters of vocal expression, but all the charm of the puppet theatre would be gone. It is even possible to dispense with puppets altogether and perform with nothing but hands–bare, gloved, or with ball-like heads; but even bare hands represent so much material that must be forged by art. It would be an equally tragic error to destroy or curtail the role of the plastic artist. It follows therefore that only in a co-operation of the two creators on an equal footing–actor and plastic artist, who must complement each other, enrich one another's art, and form a unified whole, perfectly welded together–can the future of our theatre lie. The actor, who is an agent of the laws of the theatre, imposes special forms on what is created by the plastic artist who makes puppets; and in presenting him with his puppets, the artist in his turn imposes on the actor a specific style of playing, entirely different from that which is seen on the dramatic stage.

What are the ways in which this alliance determines the characteristics of the puppet theatre?

There can be no theatre without the actor, and the actor is useless without some theatrical action developing out of a conflict, to give him characters to interpret. Now all this is impossible without a subject, without a plot, without a dramatic evolution towards a culminating point and a *dénouement*.

These are all elements which the actor brings with him from the dramatic stage and without which he cannot exist, cannot practise his art. The puppet actor brings to the puppet theatre of today the most significant innovations of the modern dramatic theatre; but, most important of all, he brings it basic, eternal qualities, without which any kind of theatre would cease to exist.

And he brings something else, something that is imperative in the dramatic theatre: a concern with the literary content of works intended for the stage. But here the actor encounters the opposition of the other member of the creative partnership, who wants a minimum of words to be used and those that are used to be taken from everyday speech, so that the characters' actions and their spiritual universe are described through the medium of physical action, the only medium the puppet possesses.

The plastic artist's demands are not limited to these. His requirements on the dramatic side go much further. Ceasing to be responsible simply for the make-up and costume of an actor, the plastic artist who creates puppets ceases to be restricted by the natural limitations of the living man—that is to say, of the actor. He ceases to be bound by them, just as the actor becomes, in the puppet theatre, independent of his physical appearance. Literally unlimited possibilities are opened up to the artist's imagination. The real face and body of the flesh-and-blood actor do not exist in the puppet theatre: there are wood, paint, papier-mâché, and many other inanimate materials which the artist is free to put together as he thinks best, achieving bold and unexpected effects. By something akin to magic, the actor will give them life through his voice and his movements. And these 'phantasms'

brought to life will in their own way serve admirably the final purpose of the theatre: *to portray human destinies, to throw into relief man's spiritual universe, to strive against evil and to sow good.*

I repeat: the final and fundamental purpose of the theatre, because to serve the people is the most important task of every form of art.

Everyone agrees that, in the puppet theatre, man's spiritual world can be represented with the help of any form, even the most fantastic. While in most cases the physical form of man himself cannot reveal his spiritual world to us and is often misleading, the plastic artist who creates puppets is able to show it to us in the most precise and convincing way.

If he wishes, the sculptor can even make a straightforward copy of a living man, of the actor. But he will only achieve a pale, anaemic imitation of the dramatic theatre—in miniature—without making any use of the specific possibilities of the puppet theatre, in all their originality. It is a truism that any copy has less value than the original and cannot properly be called a work of art.

Nevertheless many artists are forced to do this by having a dramatic plan which is entirely alien to the puppet theatre. Any work intended specifically for the puppet theatre must fulfil one vitally important condition: it must not copy the external forms of life but must reveal its essence through forms born of poetic imagination.

Let us try to divide the whole of the world's literary creation, oral and written, into two great categories: the literature of what was, or which might have been, and the literature of the fantastic, of the imaginary. Each reflects life realistically, but by radically different means. By its very nature, the puppet theatre is aphoristic, and it loves metaphorical forms and expressions; it is incapable of showing life just as it is, of soberly narrating reality, for it was created precisely to tell of what is not and what cannot be—fantasies, incredible stories in every genre: narrative, satire, poem, legend. This has never prevented it, however, from being realistic in its content, because its aim is to reflect life in order to transform it.

The Soviet people love the puppet theatre, all the more so because it is the bearer of a message for our time, full of profound social significance. This guarantees us against the attempts of certain artists to drag it onto the sterile path of formalism and would-be profound emptiness. Such a theatre would sign its own death warrant, for it would lose all its interest for the public.

The fantastic realism of the puppet theatre has nothing in common with the art that lowers man's stature and sullies him, with decadent art. For my part, I believe firmly that the partnership between actor and plastic artist must be strengthened and developed, to ensure an ever brighter future for this beautiful and wholesome art.

The Modern Puppet Stage and its Audience

by Dezső Szilágyi

Hungarian. Director of the Budapest Puppet Theatre. Originally a lawyer, and then an authority on children's literature, he has made his theatre one of the most striking in Europe.

The art of puppetry, this thousand-year-old branch of human culture, has enjoyed a kind of renaissance in our century. Its artistic means have regenerated themselves in many countries, and it has begun to attract large numbers: in Hungary, for instance, the audiences at the Budapest State Puppet Theatre reach half a million annually, making it the leading theatre in the country. To those who work in puppetry, and also to the public, one of the most interesting questions is: To what circumstances does this branch of art owe its present popularity?

What is the essence of the puppet theatre's impact on its audience? For a long time it was argued that puppetry was the ideal integrated art, the long-sought-for 'total art', and that was why it appealed to the public. True enough, this specific feature–the combination of literature, music, drama, visual art, and dancing–provides a particular enjoyment for the spectator. But the basic prerequisite for this refined aesthetic appreciation is the existence of an appropriate culture. If that is so, why then does the puppet have such an elemental and powerful impact on an unsophisticated audience, mainly on children? The answer must be that in puppetry it is not the aesthetic experience that is the primary factor but the puppet's immediate psychological impact.

Here we have to consider two factors. One is that the audience at a puppet show witnesses action which satisfies an urge present since time immemorial. On the puppet stage, before the spectator's eyes, the supreme act of creation is taking place–lifeless, dead matter is turned into life. In his own activity man, as a rule, achieves the opposite. In order to create anything he has to watch part of his living environment suffer death. To clothe himself, to make a chair, to put down his ideas on paper, to represent the world with brush and paint–to do any of these he must turn living organisms into lifeless minerals. At the same time his yearning and his wish to create life are in fact far stronger than the compulsion of his destructive instinct. This creative urge is translated into other spheres and satisfied by the puppet brought to life.

Then we have the second psychological factor of the puppet's suggestive power. In a 'living person' moving on a stage, or acting on a stage, the spectator recognizes himself, or rather he perceives his own nature. The history of mythology teaches us that long ago the puppet was the symbol of the gods and the dead, and was used only later to represent man-in-action. Psychologists maintain that the puppet is nothing other than the symbol of man himself. The puppet, therefore, no matter in what form it may appear, is, deep down in the human mind, a primordial symbol of the human being. In certain human communities it is rooted in the so-called collective unconscious; it never penetrates to the level of the conscious mind, but when it emerges it always induces the same emotions and reactions among individuals of that community. It is because of these primary psychological reactions that we view the puppet theatre in a different light from the live (human) theatre.

These general aspects, of course, manifest themselves differently among child audiences and adult audiences. An adult chancing into a puppet show for children is invariably astonished at the reaction of the audience. The children gaze on the stage as if spellbound, and their features, while they follow every action with rapt attention, reflect the full scale of real emotions. The appearance of individual puppets produces a discharge of their tension: applause, lively shouting, relieved joy (over the victory of their beloved hero). Many parents and educationists find to their amazement that even days and weeks afterwards the children recall minute details of plot or stage set which they themselves have entirely missed. Are the children really more observant than the adults?

No—the explanation instead lies in the primary effect of the puppet which we have mentioned above. The child sees himself in the puppet. The puppet represents his hopes, his motives for action. This identification with the puppet is, moreover, facilitated by the fact that a child does not perceive art passively; to a child the perception of all artistic creation is an active process in which his power of association plays an important part. The acceptance of any work of art by a child takes place, as it were, with playful ease: he places himself in the situation of the drama, in the place of the hero, and in his visual imagination acts in unison with him.

In the world of puppetry the puppet, that symbol of man, starts out by placing the model hero visually before the child's eyes; moreover, the situation is clear and the action logical. It is therefore easy for him to transpose himself into the work of art. And because the child does not yet appreciate the difference between spectacle and reality he accepts the moving and acting puppet as objective reality—even if only for the duration of the show. He plunges with blind faith into the stream of the action and puts himself in the place of the hero. His liberated imagination fills in the details and discovers new correlations of reality; his normal play activity is extended to such a degree during a puppet show that it becomes 'real' living activity. His own everyday world is thus identified with the world of art. For the child there is no division between stage and auditorium. In his imagination he enters the stage himself and transforms its abstract world into the real one.

The important thing is that, in the course of this process, of this participation, the moral values of the dramatic action are communicated to him much more effectively than if they had been transmitted in a didactic or explanatory form. It can therefore be argued that every puppet show—intentionally or not—performs an educational function from the start. Indeed, at a certain age (between four and eleven years) it is the best means of demonstrating correct attitudes.

Apart from moral education the puppet theatre is also the best tool of aesthetic education. Its integrated artistic character stimulates every kind of interest and promotes good taste. The art of the puppet theatre thus plants in the child the foundations of a visual culture that is indispensable to us today. And since puppetry does not copy reality but, in accordance with its symbolic nature, merely adumbrates it, it stimulates the imagination of the child and induces it to supplement that which he sees, thereby ensuring his participation in the show as a 'co-creator'.

And what about the adult audience? Here puppetry has not yet won its battle. The adult too is subject to the primary suggestion of the puppet, but this is not nearly enough to attract the very conscious, rational, and critically-minded modern adult to our art in the same way as we have long succeeded in doing with the instinctive, sensually orientated child audience. All over the world puppet theatres are experimenting in order to win over the condescending adult public. These endeavours are successful wherever the puppeteer not only relies on the adult's childhood memories but expresses the peculiarities of the puppet in appropriate aesthetic forms and exploits these forms consistently—that is, where he organizes his show so that the puppet signifies to the spectator a symbolic outline of human character. And when this has been achieved the puppet must not simply live in the abstract space of the stage but must also act deliberately. (Puppetry, therefore, cannot remain on the aesthetic plane of colours, shapes, and visual structures, it cannot merely remain mobile visual art. Today it can no longer content itself with a subordinate role, such as the visual illustration of a piece of music or a circus performance imitated by puppets.)

The puppet must also represent definite real and concrete human relations: it must convey "theatrical truth" in order to establish contact with an adult audience. Of course, all this looks different on the puppet stage and different again on the real stage. The puppet stage is far more a world of complete illusion. The natural homogeneity of the puppet stage—everything here is realized in the same material—does not induce in the spectator that dichotomy which is produced on the live stage by the duality of the dramatic character represented (the "human being as if") and its actor—i.e., the real live person acting on the stage. For the spectator at a puppet show there is only the puppet, not the operator. This homogeneity of the puppet stage alone is a source of aesthetic experience in an adult audience.

Another such source is the fact that the puppet—i.e., the dead matter brought to life, the human symbol—creates its own specific living space. It can act correctly only within the dimensions which the play, fantasy, and delight in conjuring have created. The puppet stage is thus the stage of human fantasy which has taken wing. Here the impossible is possible. It is the vessel of fairy-tales, dreams, and miracles, which has drifted unfettered from its moorings in reality. With its passengers it is moving towards the shores of slumbering desires, unfulfilled wishes, and sublimated beauty. And yet the puppet stage does not draw its spectator into the magic circle of abstract illusion. The puppet steeps every subject, and every object in its environment, in human life. On its stage everything becomes human.

This dual aspect of the puppet stage—freedom of illusion

and fancy and a humanizing tendency pervading all subject matter—provides a peculiar aesthetic enrichment for the adult spectator, especially in the modern puppet theatre which has already found appropriate means to express its content. The modern puppet theatre in its literary subject matter, its pictorial character, and its actions realizes a simplified stylization appropriate to the taste and the rhythm of life of present-day man. Nothing could be further from puppetry than the trend towards naturalism. Its principal aspect could be described as "reduction to the minimum and the essentials". (Hence the great success of satires and parodies staged in the puppet theatre, since the adult spectator participates directly in the artistic reduction represented by type-cast characters and situations. Moreover, he enjoys the liberating effect of comedy.)

The true means of expression of puppetry is therefore the stage metaphor. And this is not simply a question of form. With its symbolic style of performance the puppet stage makes the spectator believe that while the theatrical world may be on a separate plane, one on which the puppets are independent beings obeying their own laws, everything ultimately is rooted in the human world and therefore reflected. This impression is produced by the modern puppet theatre in the adult spectator chiefly—or so it would seem—by the application of the confrontation principle, by the simultaneous use and juxtaposition of the true and the false, the real and the unreal, the possible and the impossible, of situations, objects, and art forms. This is the best method of reminding the spectator that the unreal world of art and the reality of everyday life exist simultaneously and alongside one another. Art, in consequence, beyond mirroring or registering our real life, is also able to change it and to influence it.

Perhaps that is why puppetry is of such special importance to adults today. True, it cannot solve the great contradictions of the world outside, it cannot intervene in the struggle of material forces, but in its own modest way it can help shape the consciousness of the adult. It offers specific aesthetic experiences and, by arousing the perpetual child dormant in every adult, also has moral significance. Cynicism, apathy, fear, uncertainty, and neurosis are incompatible with the naïvely conceived but absolutely true moral message of the puppet stage.

Puppetry may lead man to this realization: he resembles not a puppet guided by somebody else's will but—to keep within the simile—the puppet operator who creates life and in so doing radiates his reality-shaping will into the world outside.

The Art of the Puppet Theatre with Special Reference to its Position in England

by Jan Bussell

English. Director of the Hogarth Puppets, deviser of Muffin the Mule, author of many books on puppetry and of personal reminiscence.

There is so much the puppet can do which the actor cannot. An author's imagination is allowed free rein. He can write about gods and about devils. His characters need not be of human shape: they can be 'things'—chairs, tables, houses, motor-cars, trees, plants—brought to life. They can be abstract figures, ideas personified—Poverty, Wealth, Anger, Love, the spirit of Fire, of Earth; or he can call in the elements—Thunder, Fog, or Sunshine—to take part. He can (very successfully) write dialogue for animals. His plays may be set in space, for his actors have no gravitational problems; or underwater, for they need no oxygen. Figures like Henry Moore's sculptures can ooze into life and tell the human race what they think of it.

A puppet is a designer's joy. In what other sphere can he dictate the shape of his actors' bodies? The puppet must be a symbol of his deepest thoughts on the character he is creating, whether expressed in the style of a cartoonist's caricature or of a poet's dreamlike fantasy. It must never be a mere replica of what he has seen, but far more than this—his comment on what he has thought. To an audience a puppet is no mere actor dressed up but a creature thought up by its designer—it really is what it purports to be. Here is a form of theatre which frees the designer as it does the author, so that his imagination may wander in strange realms of new dimensional worlds where scale is of no consequence, where a man can walk through the eye of a needle, and where microscopic organisms can perform their stellar ballets for all to see.

What is more, the whole range of the different puppet techniques is at his disposal: the slapstick comedy of glove puppets, the epic quality of rods, the mystic fantasy of shadow play, the all-round wholeness of marionettes. These very different styles can be successfully mixed in one and the same production. But a word of warning is necessary. To design a good puppet requires a sound knowledge of the construction and manipulation in all these different branches. To a puppet, movement is vital—there are many fine-looking figures hanging in exhibitions who in fact cut very feeble capers on the stage. The movement must be an integral part of the design.

But amongst those concerned with the work of a puppet theatre it is perhaps to the manipulator himself that the puppet means most. Few people stop to think much about him, yet in fact his is the performance. He is the actor. The puppet is his tool, his instrument. That is the difference between a puppet and a robot, or a mechanical doll. The puppet is being played like a musical instrument, responding to every reaction from the audience, reflecting every nuance of the actor-manipulator's interpretation. The good manipulator is not, as most people imagine, busily concerned with the details of which string to pull, which rod to push. He works the puppet as unconsciously as he works his own muscles: it becomes in fact an extension of himself. This is more obvious in the case of glove puppets where the manipulator's hand is actually inside the figure–"the puppet's soul", as Obraztsov says–but it is every bit as true of other types, even the marionettes who are more physically remote from their master on their strings. I refer here to first-class and very experienced manipulators.

A first-class manipulator is a fairly rare person. Such a man is a true actor, an artist to his fingertips. He dislikes the idea of allowing a mechanical recorded voice to dictate the tempo of his performance. Whenever possible he speaks for the puppet as he moves it, and there is no substitute that can equal this supreme feat, either for the spectator who is contributing to the mood of the performance or for the artist himself who is responding in sympathy.

Many people argue that the business of successfully recording speech for puppets is merely a matter of allowing the correct time for laughs. It is a fact, however, that a serious play with few laughs may vary enormously, not only in its general mood and feeling, but in its overall running time. It may be argued against this that a production should be so set as to dictate for the audience correct and exact reactions, allowing them no leeway of variation. But this is just the difference between film and theatre. The act of going to a live entertainment is essentially the act of sharing in and contributing to that particular performance. This live contact between artist and audience is the very essence of theatre. Even in cases where a production is performed in the same theatre each day and does not tour–where the audience may be expected to number the same and to be composed of the same type of persons–every actor will agree that each day is invariably different: to take the obvious example, a Monday audience is quite different from a Saturday audience. With the puppet show in England especially, one of its assets is the comparative ease with which it can be taken on tour; the same production may be given one day to a theatre audience of some six or seven hundred people, the next day to a small group of students at a college, and the following day in a canteen to an audience of factory workers. The reac-

tions of such different audiences in such different venues are something that no tape recorder can cope with.

With music it is another story. The tempo of music, though varying slightly from conductor to conductor, is more or less set. Puppets are particularly good dancers. Provided they employ their own steps and rhythms and do not seek to imitate their human counterparts, very fine puppet ballets can be devised; and though nothing can equal the puppet theatre's own conductor performing with a live orchestra, recorded music can become an asset if not a necessity–as it is for a champion ice skater. Opera with puppets is a more dangerous field. Ideally one would wish to see specially composed operas exploiting the puppets' special possibilities, with live singers and orchestra.

In England of late years we have considerably developed the style of marionette presentation in which the manipulator is actually seen as a shadowy figure above his puppets. Although this idea shocks some people, there is really nothing new in it, for are not those famous puppets of Japan each worked by three operators in full view? Indeed, the principal operator is generally unmasked. This does bring the manipulator a little more into the public's mind, and people are beginning to realize how he can instil his own acting personality into the puppet–for two equally good manipulators working the same puppet produce quite different results, just as no two Hamlets are the same.

Many exciting things are in fact being done with puppets up and down our country, but as yet are too little seen and known. The general public, blinded by the futile puppet films for children on television, made with electronically operated robot-like figures in photographically realistic settings with their strings cunningly concealed, is as yet unaware of the full potentiality of puppet theatre. Only the few, who have had the chance to see a first-class live performance, realize that the puppet can be a springboard to the imagination. In that lies the power which will never let it die. I predict a great revival of public interest in the years to come.

The Creative Values of Puppet Theatre

by Marjorie Batchelder-McPharlin

American. Author of many puppet books; a noted authority on creative puppetry in education, she has conducted courses on this subject all over the world.

In the puppet theatre there is unlimited scope for the imagination. Puppets may represent anything which the mind of the artist can conceive and his hands can execute. Today there are many forces which work against the natural imaginativeness of children and discourage it in adults. Education tends to develop conformity; mass entertainment, such as the cinema, radio, and television, produces audiences of spectators, not participants, while children are not stimulated to invent and make their own toys because of the great numbers of cheap ones available. Adults, too, are limited, because so much of the world's work is dull and repetitious, offering little opportunity for imagination, initiative, or originality. The arts and the handicrafts, properly used, become increasingly important in our modern world, not only as recreation for adults, but as training for children in creative thinking, without which no advance can be made in any field. But too often the art teaching to which children are exposed is formalized instead of creative.

My concern here is with the puppet theatre. What can it contribute to the needs of modern life? What is its relation to other arts? What are its distinctive qualities? When a puppet show is performed for an audience, the onlookers are spectators, as in any other form of theatrical presentation. Yet there is an intimate link between puppets and audience, which is lacking in film and television. There is complete absorption in what is happening on the stage, which may lead to spontaneous participation in the performance. But it is the puppet show which is built from the very beginning by a group of children (or non-professional adults) that provides the best release of the creative imagination. Let us think about this kind of puppet activity, especially as it relates to education.

As suggested above, the making of puppets is a problem in imaginative design, selection of suitable materials, and skill in construction. However, too much time is often spent on the technical side. Children, if given the opportunity and sufficient stimulation to start them off, will design puppets directly and quickly, using whatever materials are at hand. In early attempts especially, the results are better if freedom in developing the characters is allowed. Sometimes a 'category', such as animals, birds, people, etc., is suggested; this narrows the choice yet allows plenty of opportunity for individual designing.

With the resulting characters, an equally creative approach to play-making is possible. Here some of the techniques of creative drama may be used. It has been established that there is a child drama, as well as a child art, both growing out of the natural way in which children express themselves. When not dominated by adult concepts and demands, a child's drawing shows a kind of observation and mode of expression quite different from that of an adult. Likewise, children are natural actors. They impersonate people, machines, animals, speaking for them or making the proper sounds. They will enact whole stories, moving freely over the available space, with little need for costumes or properties, except perhaps a stick here, a bit of fabric there. If not influenced by adult ideas, there is no demand for a stage, and no desire to play for an audience.

There are no learned lines, no stiff declamatory recitations, no showing off on a stage. Instead there is opportunity for each individual to participate in playing. A clear understanding of the story to be played is essential—an action plan, upon which the dramatic structure is built. Since everyone in the group knows the play, any person can act any part. Rotation of parts is important because it allows for many interpretations of the basic action plan. The objective of creative drama is not performance for an audience, but the value to the individual which comes from participation in a group activity. Of course, playing for other children, even for adults, may come when full confidence in characterization and improvisation has been developed. The most valuable aspect of creative drama is that it is at once an individual interpretation and a group responsibility, which is basic to all theatre work. When children reach their teens, then, if they have had creative drama experience, they are prepared to enter into formal drama and they will perform much better for having had this training.

How does creative drama relate to the puppet theatre? With a group of characters made freely as suggested above, plays may be developed by the group, then acted out by individuals to practise dialogue and action. Afterwards, the puppets may be used. In working out a play in this manner, the elements of drama may be discussed, and the characters selected to portray a conflict and show action which will create suspense and lead to a climax.

These techniques were developed because it was obvious that puppets could be easily made in great numbers, but using them in dramatic situations seemed much more difficult. Play-writing is regarded as a sacrosanct art requiring special talents, and most people are reluctant to attempt it. Yet children's imagination works as well in devising dramatic situations as it does in making puppet characters. So, as stimulation for creative work with children, puppetry and creative drama are as valuable as painting, modelling, and the other arts.

By utilizing fully the inherent appeal of puppets, and by taking full advantage of all those things which puppets can do better than human actors, the puppet theatre can be a vital factor, not only in keeping alive the creative spirit, but in nurturing it in useful ways.

In addition, by incorporating the technique of creative drama, we build upon a deep-rooted human need for creative expression which we cannot afford to neglect in the mechanized and industrialized world of today.

Puppetry in Japan

by Taiji Kawajiri

Japanese. An exponent of the modern school in the Japanese puppet theatre, director of the "PUK" Theatre, Tokyo.

The history of Japanese puppetry, as far as records reveal, dates back to the tenth century, when puppets (popularly called *kugutsu*) were manipulated by wandering low-class people on the occasion of seasonal festivals and magical rites. In the following centuries, examples of this primitive art were retained in various forms among fishermen and farmers to ensure rich hauls and good crops or to charm away illness and disaster, and among townspeople—merchants and craftsmen—for festivity and amusement.

Not until the sixteenth century did the tradition of Japanese puppetry establish itself in the form of *ningyo joruri*, or musical puppetry accompanied by *joruri*. *Joruri*, some kind of musical story-telling, began to develop among low-class people in the middle of the fifteenth century, and a century later three-string instruments, introduced from the Ryukyus (Okinawa), were improved into *shamisen*, one of the most popular instruments in Japan. Accompanied by this instrument, *joruri* came to enjoy ever wider popularity, and its combination with vulgar puppetry led to the full bloom of musical puppetry (*ningyo joruri*) from the seventeenth through the eighteenth century. The best-known playwright was Chikamatsu Monzaemon (1653–1724). He is still known as the Shakespeare of Japan.

In those days one puppet was manipulated with two hands by one man behind the stage, and puppets alone were seen by the audience. Later, puppets were improved in construction step by step, and one puppet came to be manipulated by three men (robed in black from the head downward and therefore called black men) on the stage. This has since been the traditional style of Japanese puppetry widely known as *Bunraku*. This term originated from the Bunraku-Za Theatre founded in Osaka, four years after the Meiji Restoration (the end of the feudal age in Japan) or in 1872. Socio-economic conditions were such that the Bunraku-Za was the only puppet theatre opened daily at that time. Thus, Bunraku became the popular name of *ningyo joruri*.

Even Bunraku now has no theatre of its own. Moreover, it is not an independent group but is managed by the Bunraku Association, a semi-governmental organization. With its headquarters in Osaka, the Association undertakes large-scale performances in both Osaka and Tokyo and provincial performances in major cities all over the country. The Bunraku ensemble is composed of puppet manipulators, *joruri* singers, and *shamisen* players, about seventy in all.

Though the tradition of Japanese puppetry is represented by Bunraku, there are at least eighty folklore groups performing various kinds of traditional puppetry—hand puppets, rod puppets, etc. It is to be noted that Japanese hand puppets widely differ in construction from European Guignols and Punches.

The tradition of the Japanese marionette still lives in two troupes in Tokyo: Yuki and Takeda.

A New Art is Born

by Stantscho Gerdjikov

Bulgarian. Director of the Sofia Puppet Theatre, a company of marked originality which has gained the principal award at the International Puppet Festival, Bucharest.

Is it a paradox that the art of today shows growing interest in the patterns of ancient African painting and sculpture or in Japanese and Chinese engravings of old? It seems to me that strange as this interest is at first glance, it shows a definite cycle in modern development psychologically and artistically.

Nineteenth-century art was a culmination point in rendering the subject in the closest detail. The classic novelists of the last century described their characters down to their innermost being at great length. This predilection for infinite detail could be possible only if given the time and peace of mind for such introspection.

But twentieth-century life became dynamic and tense. Man's scientific thought continued to probe into the unexplored secrets of nature at lightning speed, and a formidable array of scientific discoveries has given life a new, unsettling fascination. Perhaps to keep his balance, as man plumbs the depths of scientific thought, he is disinclined to approach his emotional and artistic world in quite the same fashion as before. He prefers to restore and preserve man's emotional texture as an entity.

Perhaps as a reaction to the concentration on detail in science and industry, the tendency for simplification (in the broadest sense of the word), the tendency towards stylizing is to be observed in the life and the arts of modern man.

Once born, the new tendency rapidly proved its aptness to the dynamics and characteristic features of modern civilization. Above all, man today needs the skill to find his bearings as quickly as he can in the dizzying variety of modern life. This presupposes an ability to sift through facts, to simplify, stylize, and generalize. Expressive laconism assumes an ever greater value in the present-day communication of men. The finely shaded hint has assumed an aesthetic priority over the lavish description. Modern man is beginning to appreciate the well-selected detail which arouses a chain reaction of associations. The charming patterns of some ancient arts have recalled to today's artists and writers the aesthetic possibilities inherent in stylization and concise expressiveness.

An unsuspected creative potential was discovered in the puppet, an actor thousands of years old, for the realization of the artists' striving for a new art. The puppet has an indisputable advantage over all other actors: its innate and unlimited possibilities for stylization. The theatre puppet can execute the artist's fantasy to the full. So it is quite natural that the modern puppet theatre has gradually become a theatre of bold and original thinking in images.

The response to well-defined trends in the artistic and psychological development of modern man is one of the reasons for today's admirable revival of the ancient art of puppetry. Although its traditions are centuries old, contemporary puppet art is nevertheless a true medium for modern times. It is quite justifiable to say, therefore, that although born centuries ago, puppet-theatre art is a twentieth-century art. In the final analysis, most of the modern puppet artists have taken over from the past centuries an immortalized and poeticized human idea–the idea of personifying the essential in man. To puppet artists the efforts to discover the causes of the revival of their art are of great practical significance and of far-reaching value. I would say that this is a normal and useful road of development–the quest for the specific means of expression of the new art should proceed from the laws of theatrical culture. One should never forget that the puppet theatre is another branch of the theatre. New discoveries are not born in a vacuum.

Children 'helped' the puppet theatre win public support and popularity. This is a typical feature of the story of puppet art in a number of European countries.

In the process of creative work there came the imperceptible discovery of the affinity of the puppet stage with contemporary aesthetic trends and with modern art tastes. It was natural for the modern puppet theatre to resume vigorously its contact with adult audiences. For the time being, however, this contact is primarily on an aesthetic plane. Puppet artists are still preoccupied with the solution of new aesthetic problems. (It is not by mere chance that parodies on all aspects of the arts predominate among puppet shows for grown-ups.) As a result, the social range of the present-day puppet theatre for adults is still narrow, generally speaking; hence the search for entertainment value only.

The experience of the past teaches us that during a period of upheaval the theatre is always the noble spokesman for its times.

After having brilliantly proved its aesthetic value and independence the puppet theatre for adults now feels called upon to prove its social value and necessity. The triumph of this new art will be complete.

Voilà . . .

by Yves Joly

French. An artist who uses extremely simple means, with umbrellas, flat figures, and bare hands, to achieve results of startling dramatic effect.

Y ou make puppets; just like that, without really giving it a lot of thought–it can be done–and then one day you find yourself sitting staring at a blank sheet of paper because someone has asked you, very nicely, to describe "your creative experience and the opinions you have formed in the course of your labours". So I try to find out the whys and wherefores of this and that ... and everything starts to dissolve until I'm left with nothing ... nothing but a few incoherent ramblings, a jumble of meaningless words; the page is filled not with glowing ideas but with hideous scribbles. I am forced to yield to the evidence and admit it: I have nothing to say–I have no opinions and my experience has involved no labour–I loathe labour: I only like loving. If something is created in my hands it is not because I have decided to create it in accordance with a certain principle, or by using a certain piece of knowledge, or with a certain aim in mind–I do whatever happens to appeal to me because a force in me drives me to perform a particular action, to make a particular discovery, rather as the force of spring makes a plant shoot up and reach towards the light, towards the joy of being.

I do things to celebrate this joy when I feel it in me. If I were a dancer I should dance this joy, if I were a painter I should express it in dancing colours, and because I am neither, but have in me something of both, I find a shape and then discover how it moves. It may be very ugly or very beautiful–for others–and accordingly it either will or will not survive for the audience.

Is this a matter of creation? Can one be the creator of harmony? I can only become aware of harmony and then try to put myself in tune with it. I don't create movement; I discover it, I imitate it, I capture it, I let it live in me; day by day I discover life with its richness, its fullness, its waste, its disorder. Am I to believe that I am meant to put order into it? How boring–and where would I begin? This is the point when disorder takes over in my own mind.

Am I to give myself the right, on the strength of my own experience, to preach my own way of seeing, of choosing, of doing? But, for myself, I have rejected the experiences and successes of others; I don't like my landscape cluttered with signposts. Am I to become an educator, a teacher? But I am only a dunce myself, and usually a truant one at that. No, we must resign ourselves to the fact that I have nothing to say. If I have experience it is only a burden to me. I am only

concerned with living; with discovering life and living that discovery. Perhaps I do my discovering with puppets; that is a secret between them and me; but we have signed no contract, and perhaps because there is freedom between us there can also be love.

Between Yesterday and Tomorrow

by Carl Schröder

German (Democratic Republic). Director of the DEFA Cartoon Film Studio, Dresden; a widely experienced artist and technician.

I am asked how things are with the puppet theatre. I could answer that puppetry is about to make a big leap forward. Or I could use grandiloquent words about a renaissance of puppetry. But I do not wish to make judgments which should be left to later generations when–I hope–art historians will concern themselves with this pleasing contemplative art no less than poets and dramatists.

Instead I will talk about two visits to such theatres– theatres as fascinating as ever, yet theatres which artistically and organizationally represent diametrically opposed forms. For that very reason they illustrate clearly the present state of puppetry and the changes envisaged for the future.

Half an hour's drive out of town we came to a small village with a church, a school, and a neat village inn with a pleasant ballroom. In the adjacent farmyard stood two large trailer caravans, together with an equipment van, with the faded inscription "Ritscher's Marionettentheater". Roland, the 'principal', welcomed us with a spirited speech. He was getting on for forty, and his mother was there too. His words dropped into the space like a stage tirade, as if every sentence hung on a thread like his marionettes. In the confined space of the caravan, where the life of the puppeteer and his family unrolls year after year amidst ordinary everyday events, was a cage alive with the chirping of bullfinch, thistle-finch, and siskin. Chained up, under the chair, crouched Apollo, a setter.

Roland showed us his repertoire list: 102 plays for adults and 42 for children. What a wealth of naïve poetry written by three generations–grandfather, father, and son. Naturally these are no artistically shaped dialogues full of philosophical reflections. This is artless and simple conversation in sparse sentences. Yet content and style never lack culture. And what about the subjects? Alongside *Dr Faustus's Life and Descent to Hell* we have *The Dreyfus Affair*; alongside *Geneviève* we find the comedy of *The Captain of Köpenick*. Among the most recent productions of the big theatre the principal box-office successes have been rapidly tailored down for the marionettes. Who can say, therefore, that these popular puppet stages were not exceedingly topical and up-to-date in their day? More than that: they were the big theatre for the rural population. Admittedly, for the last few decades dramatic subject-matter has resisted adaptation to this Baroque form of theatre. The age of poachers and robbers, of princes and saints, is long past, and bombastic acting, to the point of tear-jerking, has become merely comical. As a result, only a modest fraction of the vast store of playbooks has kept to this day its intrinsic values and continued to hold its place among both the entertainment-seeking and the critical public.

Imagine more than a hundred adults sitting in front of that stage this evening, full of pleasurable anticipation. Yet the village has a population of only eight hundred. And there is a thriller on television! What then attracts these spectators to the puppet stage time and again? Perhaps it is the subjects, since the plays are mostly dramatized local legends. But more probably it is the charm of the puppets, their stilted language, the way they stride across the stage, stiffly, awkwardly, transforming and alienating reality with utterly

naïve means. The fact that the puppet is doing something it is not really able to do is what makes it so lovable. And the fact that even in its awkwardness it is so graceful produces that constant degree of amusement which leaves a smile round the spectator's lips even in a play of serious intent. The spectator's pleasure increases with the realization of the interplay of illusion and truth, with the conflict of artificiality and reality.

Is this then the whole reason why people see a puppet show? No. We have not yet mentioned the character which no poet has invented and no philosopher thought up, a character created by the people itself–Punch, the clown who belongs to the great family of Kasper, Karagöz, Petroushka, Guignol, Pulcinella, Pimperle, Karapet, or whatever else they are called, those variants of the great immortal fools and jesters the world over. It is he who has all the sympathies of the people, for he is always gay and carefree, brave and truthful, fearless and never defeated. He uses his club when his words fail to convince, and at times he is at the receiving end of the blows. But the last blow is invariably dealt out by him, for he does not die in any play. Moreover, it is he who speaks across the footlights, who holds a dialogue with the audience, who leaps out of the plot of the play, straight into the present and its problems. And all that is done with inimitable wit, quickness of repartee, and cleverness. Is such a character not the hero of our time and worth preserving?

Here you experience a truly genuine evening's theatre, naïve and light-hearted, simple as a folk-song, and when it is over you go home happy. Suspended backstage are the actors of wood and cloth, the knights and the robbers, the witches and the devil, the nobles and the villains. In the boxes, neatly arranged into sumptuous garments and underclothes, lie the costumes.

In spite of his perseverance Roland knows very well that his journey is nearing its end. Not today, and not tomorrow. The theatre is still working, and a piece of the past comes to life once more for a couple of hours in the bright glow of the footlights. But our time demands new subjects, shaped with new means of expression. Thus the theatre is already on its way to the museum; a pure Baroque itinerant theatre is nearing its end. The students of folklore must preserve whatever survives before it is lost.

And now, let us pass on to our next visit. We are standing in the town now, in front of a building dating from the turn of the century, a restaurant with dance floor, but for many years now a cinema. Above the main entrance hangs a big advertisement for the next film. On the left is a glass case with a puppet blowing a trumpet. And underneath the legend: "We are building a new puppet theatre for you!"

On the first floor are several doors. One of them says: "State Puppet Theatre". We knock and enter. The director of the theatre, formerly an actor, then a producer, and now an extramural student at the Leipzig Theatre College, welcomes us. We have come at a bad moment: sitting round a long table are the members of the company, at present twenty-five in number. On the walls are posters of puppet stages from Czechoslovakia, Poland, etc. Everything still gives the impression of improvisation, of something as yet unfinished; the company moved in only a month ago.

This puppet theatre was founded in 1952, following a guest performance by Obraztsov's theatre. It has gone through all the teething troubles of a young and inexperienced company. It was subordinated first to one big theatre and then to another; for years it had no home of its own, sharing other people's premises, on sufferance as a rule, and mostly away on tour. But they were people obsessed by their task and persevering. Now at last they have a home of their own. In the big hall is their stage—not a traditional peephole stage but one with all the facilities of up-to-date technical illusion. Free-standing and open at the top, the semicircular stage, with two performing areas, offers to the director a rich scale of patterns and arrangements. Moreover, the stage structure can be changed for other plays requiring the opposite kind of style. And what splendid puppets! Feather-light glove puppets, made of PVC film, so that even the youngest girl operators will not get tired.

Now, do you notice the fresh wind blowing here? The new style that is being born? This theatre is only twelve years old—a short period of time, but enough to show some promise of the future.

I have talked of two puppet stages, typical at this time of significant change in the movement as a whole, a movement that is made up of an abundance of effort with peak achievements and lovable naïveté, and with friendly contacts devoid of rivalry, envy, or isolation.

It is said that puppetry is as old as humanity—a happy augury for the future of this light-hearted art.

Union Internationale
des Marionnettes (UNIMA)

"UNIMA unites the puppeteers of the whole world. They regard puppetry as an art which brings all countries together, an art addressing itself both to children and to adults. The members of UNIMA wish to place their art at the service of peace throughout the world." – Preamble to the UNIMA Statute

by Max Jacob

German (Federal Republic). President of UNIMA. A distinguished puppeteer, who was largely responsible for raising the traditional folk Kasperl theatre to the level of a significant artistic and educational medium.

For a long time and in all countries puppetry has been a thing of the people. Among many civilized nations, throughout long periods of history, it made its contribution to intellectual development. For that reason it will always live, even though some critics question its viability. During the past fifty years puppetry has experienced a new lease of life, and especially in the years following the two world wars has it attracted fresh attention.

From the beginning our eyes had been turned towards the Czechoslovak puppeteers who were blazing the trail for our art. It was no coincidence therefore that UNIMA was founded in that ancient cultural centre, Prague, in 1929. The idea of some international link-up had been mooted for some time. The pros and cons had been examined in countless discussions among leading puppeteers and puppetry supporters, usually at national congresses, until in May 1929 the invitations went out for the constituent congress of UNIMA to be held in Prague. The first President of UNIMA was Professor

Dr Jindřich Veselý, and its first Secretary-General Václav Sojka-Sokolow.

Later that same year, in November 1929, the second UNIMA congress was held in Paris. The number of member States at first was not very large; the international ties had yet to be forged. The first members came from Czechoslovakia, Germany, France, England, Belgium, Italy, Switzerland, Hungary, and the U.S.A.

From the very start UNIMA did not consist merely of "fully paid up members" who believed that membership would mean for them the dawn of a financial golden age. They were all conscious of helping in the building of something that would one day act as a powerfully radiating centre. UNIMA never had any political ambitions, but its motto "Peace on Earth" invariably dominated its work. The spirit of toleration, based on mutual respect, has remained to this day the principle governing all its members, no matter in what country and in which continent they live.

In September 1930 UNIMA convened its third congress in Liège, and its fourth congress was held in Ljubljana (Yugoslavia) in July 1933. There, UNIMA elected Professor Josef Skupa to be its new President. Together with him, Professor Jan Malík, of Prague, was elected to be the new Secretary-General, and he has held this difficult office to this day, a period of more than thirty years, discharging it responsibly and ably. Members consider themselves fortunate that Prague has in this way remained the seat of UNIMA ever since its foundation. Ljubljana was the venue of the last congress before the Second World War. A few other countries had joined by then: Bulgaria, Austria, Poland, Yugoslavia, the Soviet Union. Thus UNIMA had fourteen member States just before the war.

The years of political tension preceding the Second World War made international co-operation in UNIMA increasingly difficult, and during the war it came to a halt altogether. As far as possible members in different countries, if they were personal friends, maintained contact with one another, but no country could be induced to convene a congress; the barriers were insuperable. Even after the war the international co-operation of puppeteers could not be resumed immediately. The damage done in all fields was too frightful; nations had drifted too far apart. It was many years before the threads could be taken up again. Professor Malík, the Secretary-General of UNIMA, was indefatigable in his efforts to restore the former contacts between puppeteers in different countries and to create new ones.

In March 1957 the city of Brunswick in Germany organized the first Week of European Puppetry since the war. For the first time puppeteers from East and West met again; performances were given by German puppet theatres as well as by theatres from Switzerland, Austria, Czechoslovakia, France, and Sweden. The latest puppet films from many countries were shown. Professor Malík had come from Prague with several friends. It was clear from many conversations that the time had come to revive UNIMA. But one exceedingly grievous loss had been suffered: Professor Josef Skupa, its President, an internationally famous puppeteer and the creator of the world-renowned puppets Father Špejbl and his son Hurvínek, had died in January 1957 after a grave illness. Professor Malík sent out invitations to the fifth congress to be held in Prague from 7th to 14th December 1957. This was an event of far-reaching importance in the world of puppetry. In spite of the unfavourable time of year some 200 participants turned up, including 78 from abroad. UNIMA elected a new praesidium. The new President was Max Jacob of Hamburg, the Vice-Presidents were Sergei Obraztsov (U.S.S.R.) and Dr Vittorio Podrecca (Italy).

The meeting unanimously approved the following declaration: "Puppeteers from sixteen countries have met in Prague for the fifth congress of the Union Internationale des Marionnettes (UNIMA). Proceeding from the tradition of this organization, originally founded in 1929, they heard extensive reports by the various delegations on the present state of the puppet theatre and examined its opportunities of further development on an international plane. The plenary session of the congress addressed itself to puppeteers throughout the world with the urgent appeal to initiate, strengthen, and develop mutual international relations in their field

and, while fully respecting the peculiarity of national traditions, to create a truly contemporary puppet theatre which would serve the ideas of humanity, international co-operation, and peace."

Anyone who has followed the development of puppetry from 1957 to this day or who has seen and experienced the many splendid weeks of puppetry festivals will know that puppeteers throughout the world have gone a long way towards implementing this declaration. From one congress or festival to the next the part which puppetry is playing in the theatrical life of our age has become increasingly clear. Numerous bold experiments have led to new stylistic forms, new techniques, and a new concept of production. A great deal of careful study and loving understanding has been spent on a child's requirements for his intellectual and emotional development. Whatever was inadequate or unsuitable has been eliminated. Puppetry, as a result, has become a basic preparation for the theatrical experience of young people in many countries, just as much as an independent artistic institution in the life of children and juveniles.

Moreover, new developments have increasingly been making themselves felt in the field of puppetry for adults. The influences upon one another of the visual art of our century and a multitude of formal, stylistic, and scenic developments in puppetry have clearly emerged.

Of considerable importance is the international cross-fertilization that is made possible by the meetings organized by UNIMA. These provide the organizational framework and the solid foundations for artistic and intellectual exchanges, for promising future developments. The fact that close human contacts and personal friendships are forged, or that intellectual disputes are settled peacefully, is due less to the programme of UNIMA than to the happy opportunities arising from these meetings.

In May 1958 the "First International Puppetry Festival" was held in Bucharest. This proved a great success. Simultaneously, within the framework of this festival, the sixth UNIMA congress was held. This was exceptionally well attended, and the number of member States and individual members grew considerably. Reports on educational and artistic aspects of puppetry produced lively discussions.

In June 1959 the second UNIMA conference was held in Paris; simultaneously a number of internationally famous puppet theatres gave guest performances as part of the annual "International Theatre Festival" at the Théâtre des Nations.

In Paris the UNIMA praesidium had before it invitations from Bochum and Brunswick, both these cities offering to be the host for the seventh UNIMA congress in March 1960. Both invitations were accepted, and thus it came about that, for the first time, a UNIMA congress was held in two places: first in Bochum from March 22nd to 24th, 1960, and subsequently in Brunswick.

In September 1960 Bucharest was host to the "Second International Festival" which was again a meeting of theatres from all over the world. Simultaneously the third UNIMA conference was held and many specialized reports were given and discussed. The impetus given to puppetry by the revival of UNIMA was shown also by the "International Puppetry Festival" in Rome, organized officially by the Italian Government and under the patronage of UNIMA; this was held at the Teatro Valle from June 18th to 25th, 1961. Linked with this festival was the fourth UNIMA conference at the Villa Falconieri in Frascati, with interesting papers and discussions on puppetry for children of all ages. Simultaneously a meeting was held of the UNIMA praesidium.

The fascination which the words 'UNIMA' and especially 'UNIMA congress' have for its members throughout the world was shown again by the eighth UNIMA congress, staged so splendidly in Warsaw from June 18th to 25th, 1962. Several hundred participants had arrived from about twenty-five countries to take part in this festive occasion.

Simultaneously with the eighth congress the fifth UNIMA conference was held.

Thanks to the work of UNIMA and to the efforts of well over 1000 members in more than forty countries, puppetry as an art has experienced a popularity and public recognition as never before. The puppeteers are forging bridges between nations; they are among their countries' best ambassadors, because they speak in the language of fairy-tale and fancy, a language understood the world over. This is reflected also in the fact that since 1960 UNIMA, on the strength of its work, has been a regular member of the I.I.T. (Institut International du Théâtre) and hence affiliated to UNESCO.

At the end of November 1962 the praesidium met in Budapest for its tenth regular working session and simultaneously observed there the fifteenth anniversary of the Budapest State Puppet Theatre. Throughout a whole week this theatre showed its best productions, a different one each day. This Budapest theatre combines the traditional and the modern so successfully that in spite of a predominantly fairy-tale character each production radiates a kinship with our own day.

The first international puppetry festival in Britain was held at Colwyn Bay from May 20th to 25th, 1963, under the patronage of UNIMA. This event again testified to the importance attached by puppeteers from all lands to meetings of this kind: visitors were present from numerous countries. No individual tours or guest performances can afford to a company the same opportunity or the same wealth of international exchanges as that provided by international meetings and congresses. There they witness the work of the great reformers of puppetry, there they collect ideas for their own work.

These meetings, however, are by no means confined to professional puppeteers; they are attended by numerous amateurs from all over the world, many of whom have given evindece in their productions of their high degree of skill.

Professor Dr Jindřich Veselý, the first President of UNIMA, wrote in 1932: "Every international association is, first of all, important within its own field—that of the puppeteers for puppetry. But every such association represents at the same time a new link in cultural work and hence has wider significance. The more such points of contact we have, the more ideas are exchanged between different nations, the better our personal contacts, co-operation, tolerance, friendship, and solidarity, the nearer shall we approach the ideal of friendly coexistence of all nations."

International Artistic Meetings

by Henryk Jurkowski, Margareta Niculescu, and Harro Siegel

When international puppet-theatre festivals appeared on the post-war artistic scene they reflected a desire to draw the nations closer together, to communicate primarily in the language of culture and art, in order to help create a climate of beauty and serenity in the world.

Puppeteers have always remained faithful to the idea of international cultural co-operation, ideals which they adopted and formulated themselves many years ago in the UNIMA programme.

So it was no coincidence that the first puppeteers' conference after the war (European Puppetry Week–Brunswick, 1957) took place in the same year as the rebirth of UNIMA (Prague, December 1957).

Nor is it by chance that most of the international festivals in subsequent years have been connected with UNIMA conferences and congresses. Thus the festivals have become a part of this organization's regular activities. Their aims correspond exactly to those upheld and promoted by UNIMA.

Among these internationally important events, two have become permanent, regular fixtures. Both have been going on for some years, and their importance is confirmed by the intense interest shown by puppet enthusiasts throughout the world: they are the Brunswick Puppet Theatre Week, held in 1957, 1960, and 1963 (founded and organized by Professor Harro Siegel) and the Bucharest International Festival (held in 1957, 1960, and 1965); to them goes the credit for stimulating other festivals and other meetings at a professional level and on an international scale. Thus they

have acquired a reputation as events of the highest importance, exerting a considerable attraction even among those not connected with puppets.

The festivals have become a meeting place for puppeteers from different countries, where the work of a wide variety of artists is juxtaposed, and where men meet together and collaborate. They have come to play a considerable part in the development of the art of puppetry–and many professional articles and discussions, and even plays created in different parts of the world, reflect the exchange of opinions and of artistic techniques to which these meetings give rise.

The first festivals tended mainly to show representative programmes: the puppeteers remembered past relationships, past successes, past partnerships long since interrupted and which demanded to be renewed. This impression is confirmed by the programme of the Liège Festival (1958), at which two groups emerged: the traditional and the modern.

Traditions in puppetry acquired new significance with the establishment of points of contact between the modern art theatres and the popular puppet forms. The latter have inspired artists and their creations for centuries, thus constituting a proof that the cultural heritage of the world's puppet theatres is a permanent one and that this broad branch of art has its value in the present as well as in the past. Twelve traditional groups have reaffirmed the inexhaustible vigour of puppet tradition, whose ancient themes still retain all their original freshness. In the above-mentioned programmes, plays were featured which used well-known heroes or famous techniques: Guignol, Lafleur, Hänneschen, Punch, or the puppet heroes of Sicily.

These are only some of the historical arguments in favour of the continuity of the art of puppetry.

The first festivals also introduced certain puppet theatres which attained great fame and popularity between the two world wars, and which enriched the art with qualities brought by the great wave of theatrical revival at the beginning of this century.

So it was with Professor Skupa's Špejbl and Hurvínek Theatre of Prague (Brunswick, 1957), with Sergei Obraztsov's

Moscow Central Puppet Theatre (Bucharest, 1958), and with the theatres of Vittorio Podrecca, Aicher, Max Jacob, Zaloziecki, Blin, Chesnais, Harro Siegel, and many others whose contributions formed a real bridge between the beginning of the century and the present day. For the post-war generation of young puppeteers programmes of this sort, conceived on historical lines, constituted excellent schooling in the artistic traditions of puppetry.

This was all the more important and necessary because there appeared in Europe some entirely new theatrical centres, which steered clear of known traditions and well-trodden paths. The originality of the theatres of Rumania and Poland, and later of Bulgaria and Hungary, was enhanced by comparison with the old concepts.

In those countries which hardly figured in the art of puppetry before the war, movements developed with new artistic values brought in by producers, writers, and performers who had used their intelligence and their talent to profit from the favourable material conditions created by state support, giving free rein to their new vision of their art. This explains how the Rumanian puppet theatre was able to make such a considerable contribution to the success of the Bucharest Festival and to ensure that it occupied a central place among subsequent international events. In the same way the diversity of methods and the creative exuberance of the Polish puppet theatre became the characteristic qualities of the Warsaw International Festival (June 1962), an event which unquestionably enjoyed enormous popularity.

Festivals have fulfilled their aim of encouraging mutual inspiration not only by the natural method of introducing artists to one another and of showing their plays, but also by providing an atmosphere favourable to innovation. Even at the first Brunswick Festival new positions were adopted which foreshadowed contemporary trends in the art (Fred Schneckenburger, Harry Kramer).

The 1958 Bucharest Festival offered a veritable feast of innovation. A positive parade of varied and expressive methods was seen there, all sharing the common desire to break away from the methods of the live theatre.

The theatre of 'hands', with or without coloured gloves, the poetry of cut-out cardboard shapes, whose scope extends from burlesque to high tragedy (Yves Joly's French company, the style of theatre described as "without characters", which uses highly original masks), the "Groteska" Theatre of Cracow, the play which uses a combination of actors and puppets (the Warsaw "Lalka" Theatre's *The Troubles of Guignol*), the play in which the idea takes on a very expressive plastic form, and the roles of puppet and décor are fused in order to intensify the parody (the Bucharest "Tandarica" Theatre's play *Hand with Five Fingers*)—each of these plays has blazed a new trail and suggested other courses, all leading directly away from the traditions of the dramatic theatre.

More recent festivals too have revealed this continual experimentation with new methods. At the Bucharest Festival of 1960 the wordless puppet show based on Prokofiev's *Peter and the Wolf*, by the Central Puppet Theatre, was also a great success. And the 1962 Warsaw Festival confirmed the effectiveness of masks, in the "Lalka" Theatre's *The Little Tiger Pietrek*; here the living image moved against a flat background, and the influence of the cinema was apparent. It was on this occasion too that the new 'black theatre' technique was presented, as was the actor-puppet combination.

Naturally, experiment is as exacting in the puppet theatre as it is in the live theatre, and the success of an experiment is just as difficult to achieve. The programme given by the German group "Die Klappe"–sober mime expressed in extremely severe plastic terms, almost ascetically–which was first shown at Bochum in 1960, provoked little real enthusiasm until the Warsaw Festival of 1962.

There is no doubt that international festivals have proved their value in drawing attention to the experiments which add to the variety of the art, give it vitality, and increase its appeal, though these festivals must not become the only criterion, the puppeteers' sole concern.

The festivals have also applauded unanimously moments of incomparable artistic worth provided by such masters of puppetry as Sergei Obraztsov, Albrecht Roser, Carl Schröder, Jan Bussell, and many others. In the individual programmes of these artists, who express themselves in a style well known in what might be called the classical puppet theatre, there was apparent a freshness, a constant vitality, maintained by the sense of values, the lively wit, the talent, and the virtuosity of those who presented them. As far as virtuosity is concerned, the same can certainly be said of the Chinese puppet shows which received such well-deserved applause at the Bucharest Festival of 1960.

All the festivals have also provided ample opportunities for the discussion and study of the educational possibilities of puppets.

The Rome Festival (1961) presented much that was worthy of attention, especially the work of artists who aim at the child audience; we shall mention only Jean-Loup Temporal, who establishes contact with his young spectators by the use of very simple yet subtle images, and the musical productions of the "Opera dei Burattini" directed by Maria Signorelli.

One of the last chronologically, but certainly not least in importance, variety, and impact, was the festival of Colwyn Bay, Wales (1963).

The London Festival revealed the many facets of the English puppet theatre, from the traditional show of the famous Punch and Judy man Percy Press to the sensitive and poetic repertoire of Waldo and Muriel Lanchester. Participants from other countries also used a variety of different methods–and we must pass over a great many and mention here only the intellectual puppet theatre, concerned with the philosophical problems of our day.

Interest in the international festivals has now spread beyond the frontiers of Europe. It is true that only a comparatively small number of the 179 groups and individual artists who took part in international festivals between 1957 and 1963 were from other continents, but of those there were we must mention the productions by the student group from Indonesia, by the Argentine group, those by artists from Japan, India, and Rhodesia, and those by the young puppet theatre of Cairo. At Brunswick and Colwyn Bay the American puppeteers George Latshaw and Daniel Llords took part for the first time in European festivals.

True to the principles of UNIMA, groups of amateurs also take part in the festivals; this enables them to benefit from the example of the professional theatres, while the professionals in turn enjoy the freshness and originality which characterize amateur productions.

It is also worth noting the sustained interest which has been shown over the years in the festivals for amateurs traditionally held at Chrudim (Czechoslovakia) and Bochum (West Germany), and which resulted in 1964 in the holding of a great international festival for amateur puppeteers at Karlovy-Vary (Czechoslovakia).

International puppeteers' festivals invariably create an atmosphere of friendliness and co-operation, of shared delight in the international art of puppetry.

Despite the diversity of the languages in which puppeteers express themselves, their art, which has always been an art of travelling performers, expresses itself in a language which is within the comprehension of everyone, as it has the power of reflecting the nobler aspirations of the whole of humanity.

PLATES

2, 3

4, 5

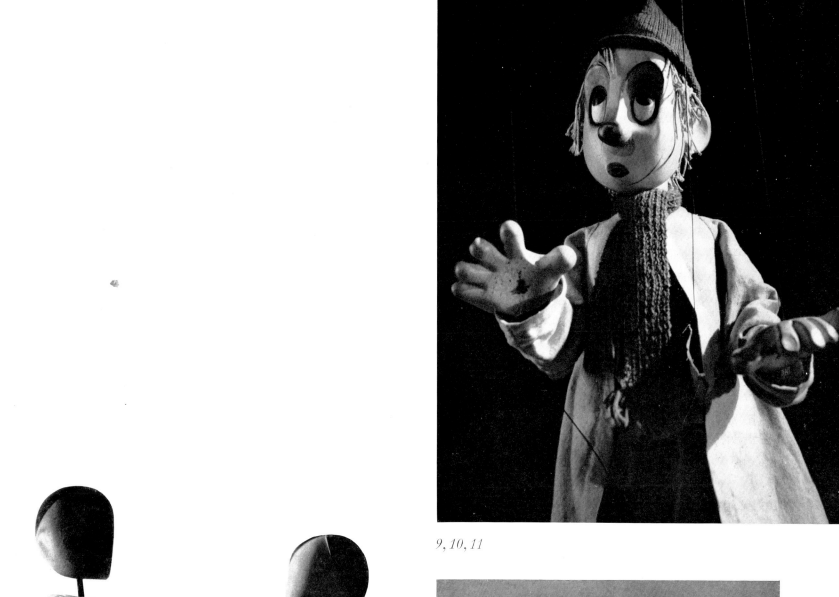

9, 10, 11

12, 13

14

15, 16

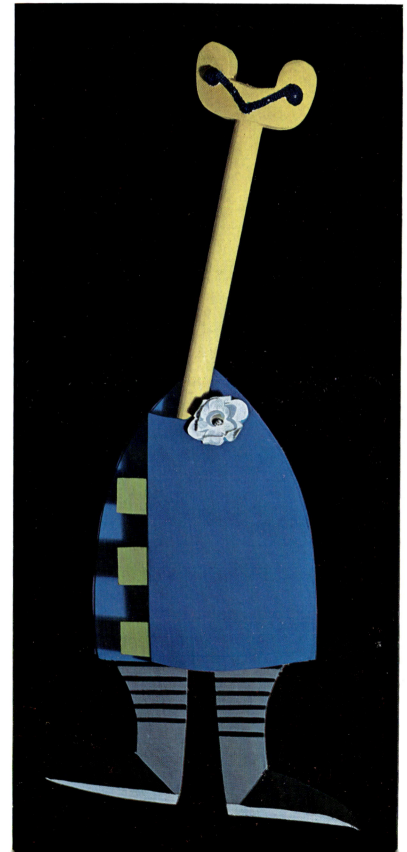

17

20, 21

22, 23

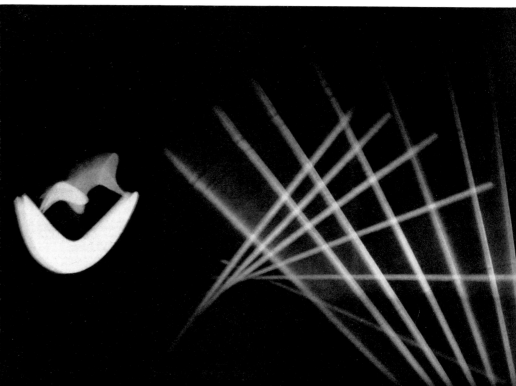

25, 26

27, 28

32, 33

34, 35

36, 37

38, 39

40, 41, 42

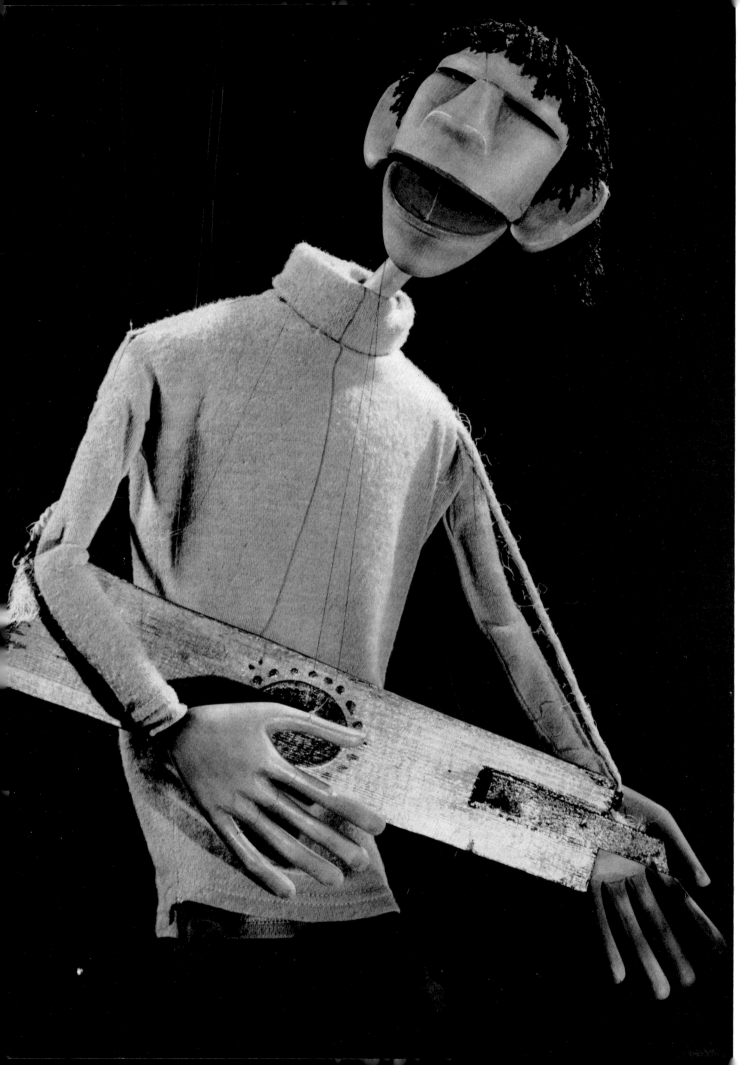

44, 45

46, 47

48, 49

51, 52

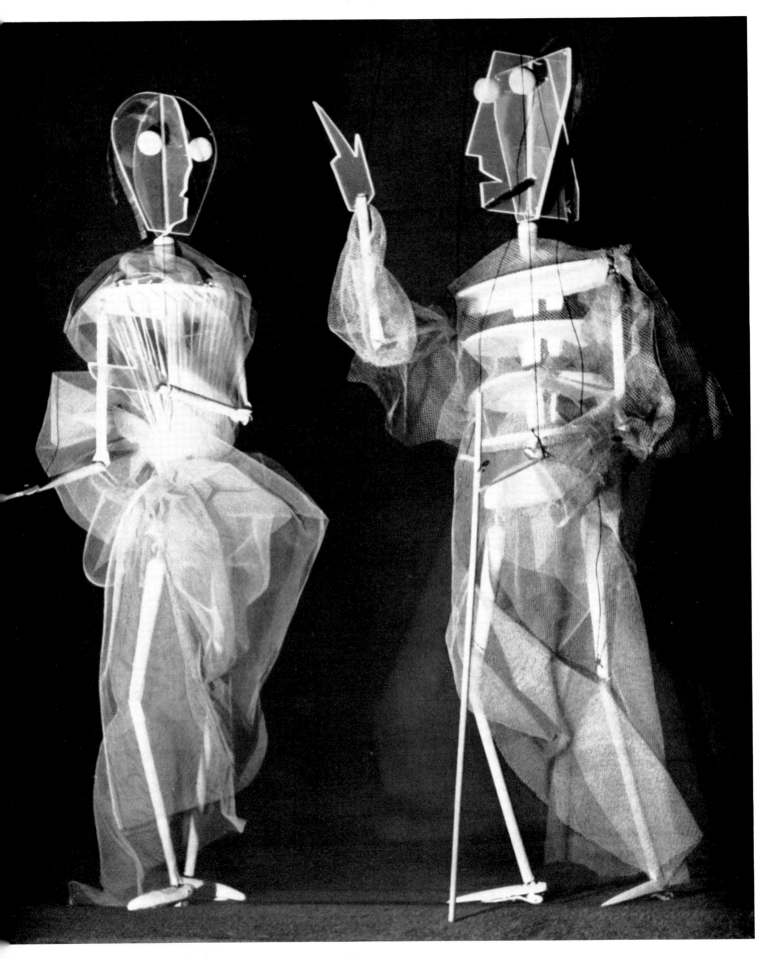

55, 56, 57

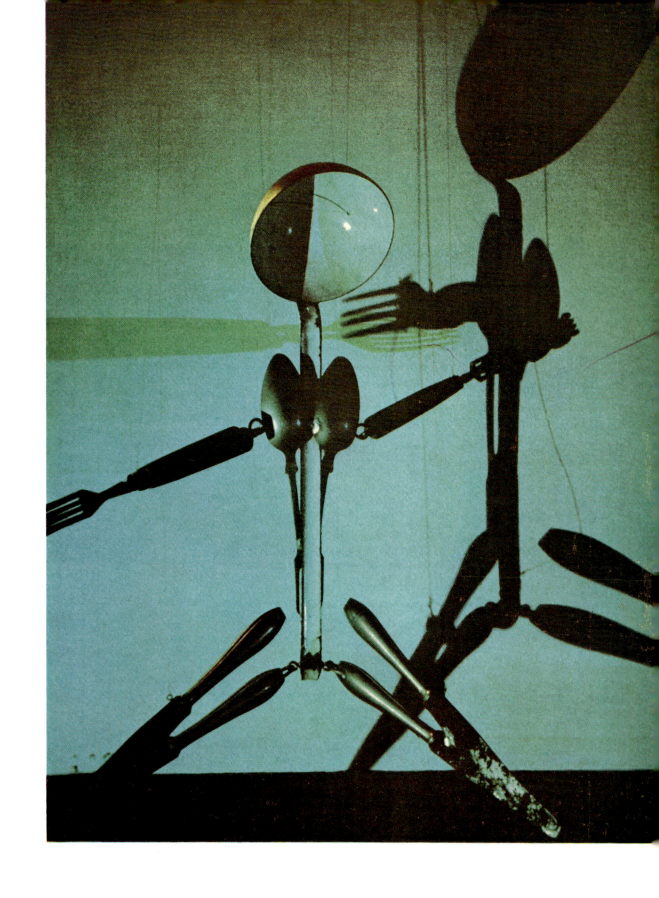

60, 61

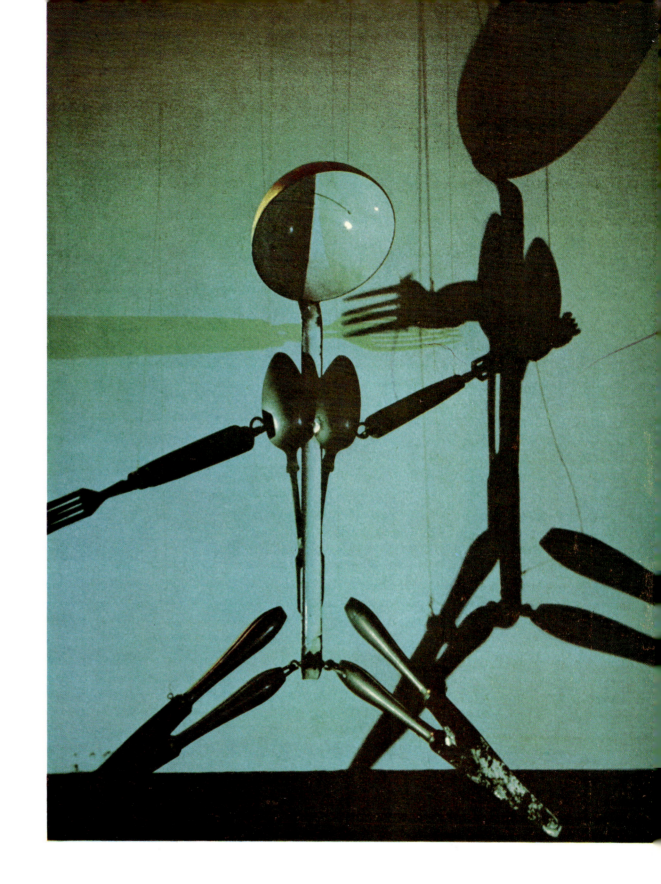

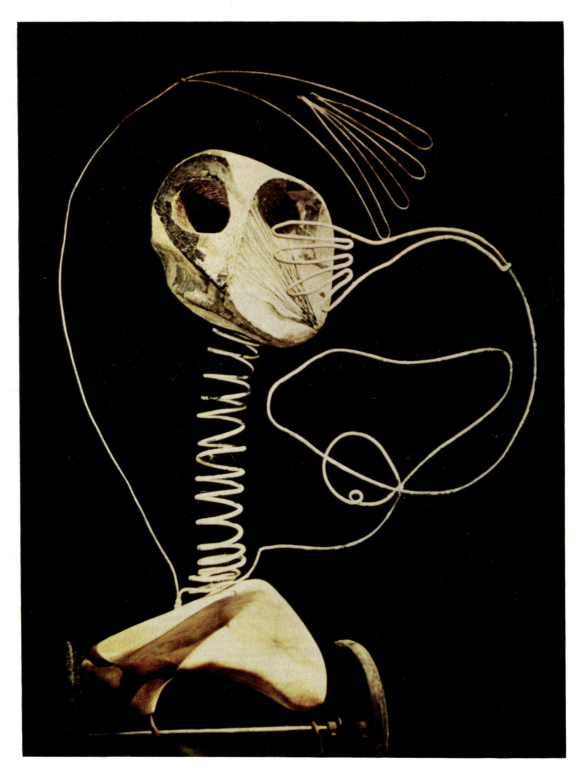

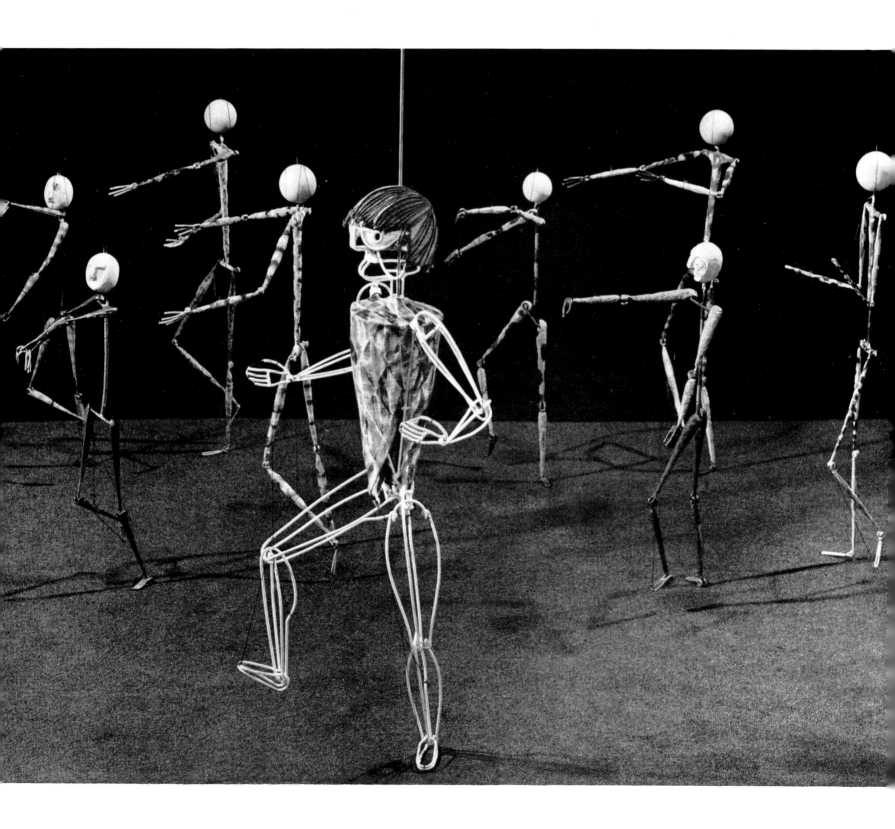

60, 61

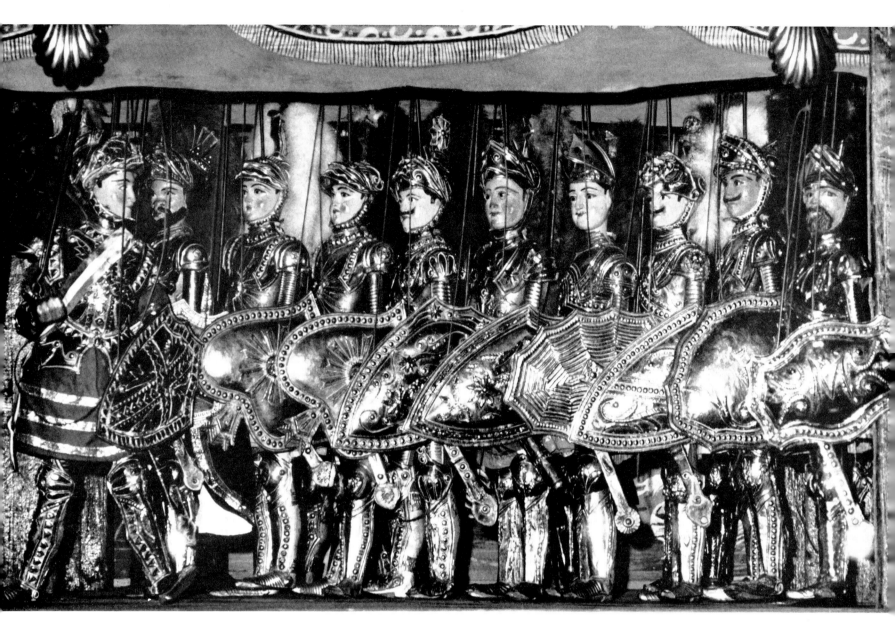

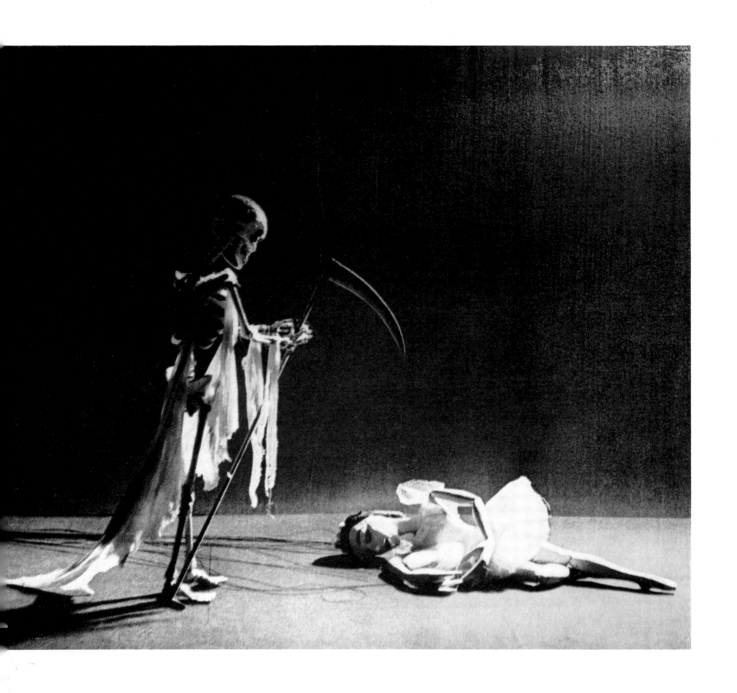

63, 64, 65

66, 67

69

70, 71

72, 73

74, 75

78, 79, 80

81, 82

84, 85

87, 88

93, 94

87, 88

89, 90

91, 92

93,94

95, 96, 97

98, 99

102, 103, 104

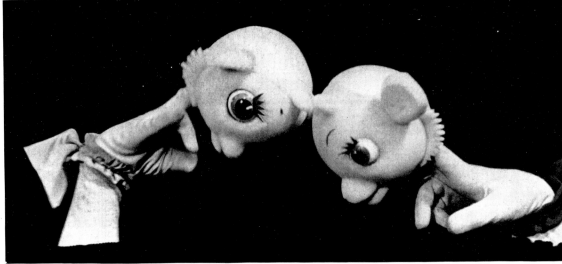

105, 106, 107

112, 113

114, 115

116, 117

118

123, 124

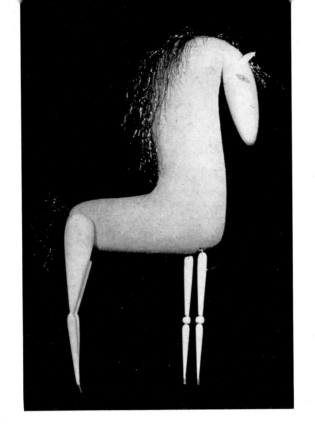

125, 126

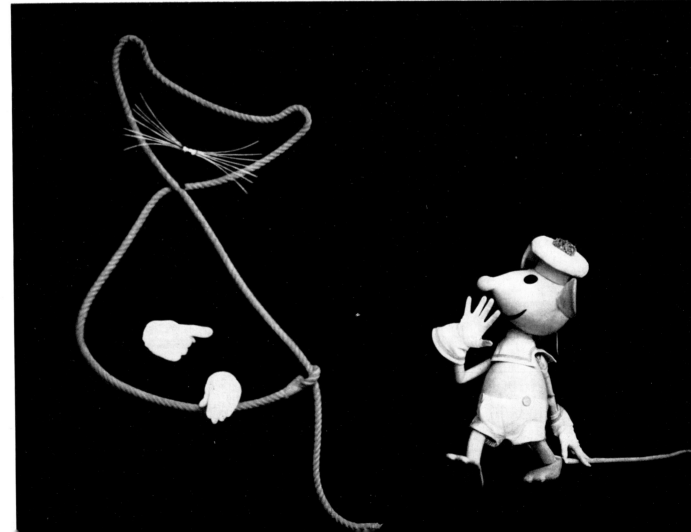

127, 128

127, 128

129, 130, 131

132, 133

142, 143

144, 145, 146

147, 148

149, 150

153

154, 155

157, 158, 159

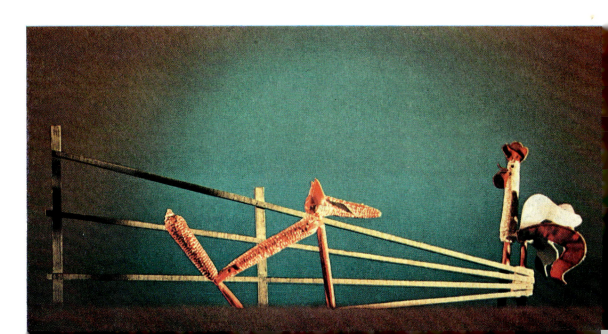

160, 161

162, 163

165, 166

167, 168, 169

178, 179

167, 168, 169

170, 171

172, 173

175, 176, 177

178, 179

180, 181

182, 183

194, 195

198, 199, 200

202, 203

208, 209

210, 211

212, 213, 214

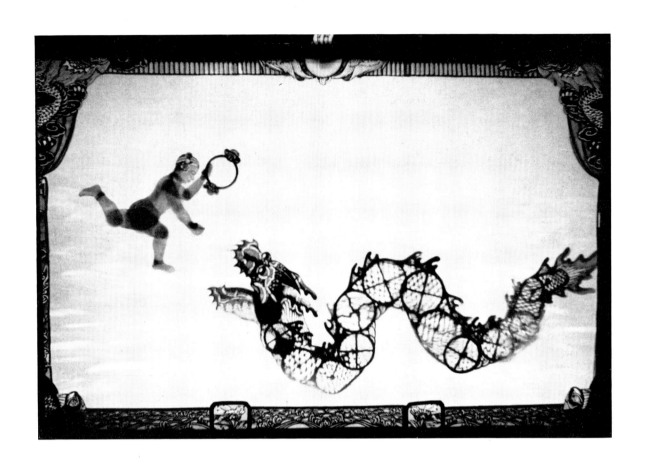

215, 216, 217

220, 221

222, 223

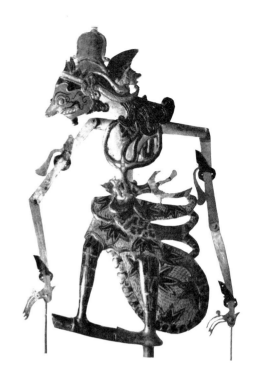

224, 225, 226

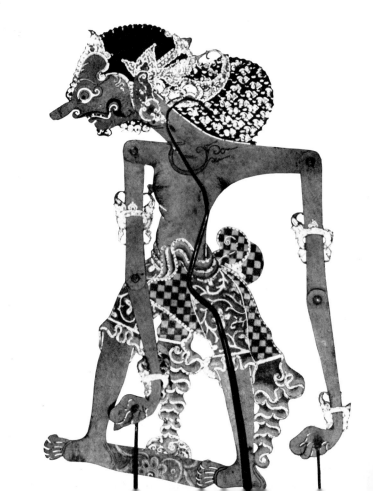

227, 228, 229

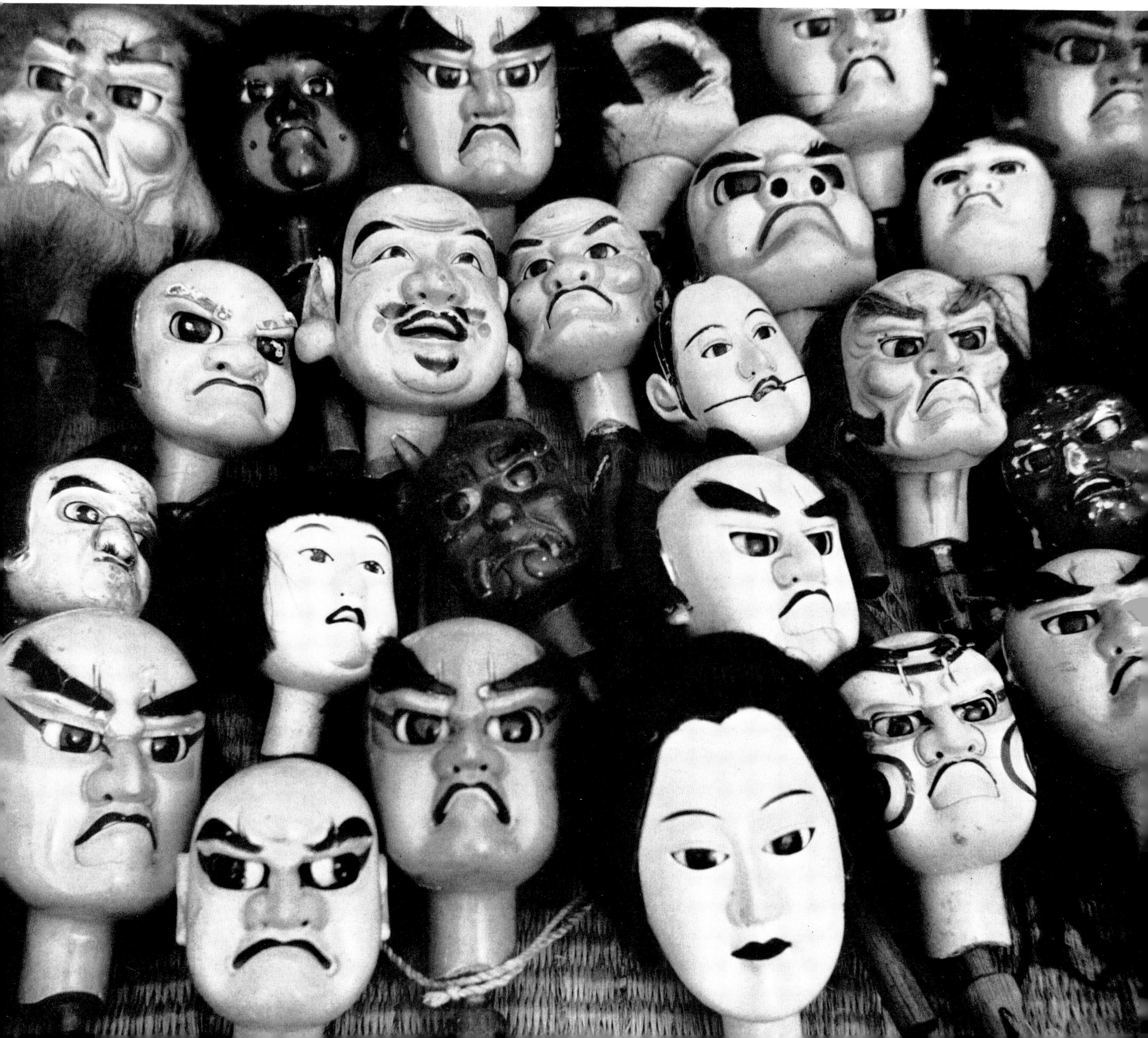

231, 232

233, 234, 235

236, 237

238

Britain

1 Percy Press booth at B.P. & M.T.G. summer school 1960. Illustration: Mr Punch and Joey (traditional characters)

2 The Little Angel Theatre, London. *Creation*, a fantasy by Lyndie Parker and Wolfgang Manthey. Producer: John Wright. Stage design: Lyndie Parker and Wolfgang Manthey. First performance 1962

3 Violet Philpott Puppet Theatre. *The Egg*, by Violet Philpott. Puppets: Violet Philpott. Illustration: Bandicoot

4 The Troubadour Puppets. *Conflict*, an African subject. Puppets: Elizabeth J. Coleman

5 Jane Phillips Caricature Theatre. Illustration: Miss Junk

6 The Lanchester Marionettes, Stratford. *L'Amfiparnasso*, a madrigal opera. Puppets: Waldo S. Lanchester

7 The Hogarth Puppets, London. *El Retablo de Maese Pedro*. Illustration: Charlemagne's court

8 Harlequin Puppet Theatre, Colwyn Bay. Puppets: Eric Bramall. Illustration: Two harlequins

9 John Blundall Puppet Theatre. Illustration: Harlequin and Columbine. Rod puppets by John Blundall

10 The Little Angel Theatre, London. *John Bellman*, by Johan Fabricius. Puppets: John Wright and Jane Tyson. First performance 1953. Illustration: Bumble, a character appearing in nearly every one of John Wright's puppet shows

11 John Blundall Puppet Theatre. *The Adventures of Pod*, by John Blundall. Puppets: John Blundall. Illustration: Pod

12 The Little Angel Theatre, London. *Lancelot the Lion*, by Margaret Marshall and Joseph Nicolson. Puppets: Lyndie Parker and Christopher Leith. First performance 1963. Illustration: Mr Crayfish, Martha, and Percy

13 *The Happy Prince*, by Lotte Reiniger. Illustration: The seamstress and the child

14 Illustration: Phoebe and Geronimo. Puppets by Martin Granger (for cabaret and variety shows). Geronimo with his bow and arrow hits a target very accurately at five yards

France

15 Compagnie Yves Joly, Paris. *Paper Tragedy*

16 Compagnie Jean-Loup Temporal, Paris. *Negative*, a sketch by Jean-Loup Temporal. Puppets: Philippe Sarazanas and Janine Antonnucci. Music: Michel Fuste-Lambezat. First performance 1962

17 "Marionnettes du Manigole", Paris. Illustration: The man Gusée

18 Robert Desarthis's Théâtre de Jardin du Luxembourg, Paris. Illustration: Aladdin Pasha

19 Compagnie André Tahon, Paris. *The Papotin Revue*. Illustration: Nathalie

20 Georges Tournaire and Robert Gouge Marionettes, Paris. *Necktie Circus*. Illustration: The banjo player

21 Claude and Daniel Bazilier Marionettes, St Denis. Illustration: Bastille day

22 Youth Theatre in Amiens (Somme). *Jeux de mains*, a modern fantasy by Lucien Caron

23 Georges Lafaye Puppet Theatre, Paris. *Tempo*, by Georges Lafaye. Production and stage design: Georges Lafaye

24 "Les P'tits Bonshommes d'André Blin", Montrouge (Seine). *Captain Fracasse*, by Théophile Gautier, adapted by Lucienne Goubat. Production and stage design: André Blin. Puppets: Lucienne Blin. First performance 1952

25 "Arc en ciel" Puppet Theatre. *The Devil*, by Geza Blattner. First performance 1944

Belgium

26 Toone Theatre, Brussels. Illustration: Belgian folklore scene

27 Toone Theatre (Toone VII), Brussels. *The Passion*, by Michel de Ghelderode. Puppets: Jose Géal (Toone VII). Illustration: St Michael and the Devil (Lucifer)

28 Fanchonnet Marionette Theatre, Brussels

Switzerland

29 Zurich Marionettes, Fred Schneckenburger. Illustration: The Over-Correct Man (cast in a mould)

30 Zurich Marionettes, Fred Schneckenburger. Illustration: Kasperr

31 Therese Keller, Münsingen. Illustration: Fritzi and the spide

Netherlands

32 "Merlijn" Puppet Theatre, Haarlem. *Spiegel, the Kitten*, after Gottfried Keller, adapted by Margreet Boldingh. Production, puppets, and stage design: Rien Baartmans and Maaike Baartmans-Hobbel. Music: Dick Mandersloot. First performance 1963. Illustration: Two gravediggers

33 Guido van Deth Puppet Theatre, The Hague. *Suuske and Her Little Donkey*, by Guido van Deth. Production and stage design: Guido van Deth. Puppets: Livinus van de Bundt. First performance 1962. Illustration: Barabbas, the villain, and Piccardan, the policeman

34 Pieke Dassen's "Die Blauwe Scuyte" Puppet Theatre, Maastricht. *Esmoreit*, a medieval play. Production, puppets, and stage design: Pieke Dassen. First performance 1962. Illustration: Princess Damiet

35 Pieke Dassen's "Die Blauwe Scuyte" Puppet Theatre, Maastricht. *The Ghost*, by Pieke Dassen. Production, puppets, and stage design: Pieke Dassen. First performance 1962

Norway

36 Oslo Puppet Theatre. *The Animals in the Hakke-Bakke Forest*, by Torbjörn Egner. Production: Alfred Solaas. Puppets and stage design: Torbjörn Egner. First performance 1959. Illustration: Fox, mouse, and elk

37 As 36. Illustration: The mouse Kaltremus

Sweden

38 Michael Meschke Marionette Theatre, Stockholm. *Nocturne II*, a pantomime by Michael Meschke. Puppets: Michael Meschke. Stage design: Gilbert Regazzoni. First performance 1957

39 Michael Meschke Marionette Theatre, Stockholm. *The Space Pioneer*, by Bo Setterlind. Production and puppets: Michael Meschke. Stage design: Gilbert Regazzoni. First performance 1961

Finland

40 Helsinki Dock Theatre (Helsingin Nukketeatteri). *The Invisible Hand*, colour film. Puppets: Mona Leo. First performance 1962. Illustration: Prince in the dead forest

41 Helsinki Dock Theatre (Helsingin Nukketeatteri). Illustration: Saturnus, also The Monster (Mona Leo puppet, 1951)

42 As 41. Illustration: Princess (Mona Leo puppet)

Federal Republic of Germany

43 Albrecht Roser's Marionettes, Stuttgart. *Marionette Cabaret*, by Albrecht Roser. Production and puppets: Albrecht Roser. Illustration: The Rat Catcher (solo marionette)

44 As 43. Illustration: Gustaf the clown

45 Puppet stage of Stuttgart youth centres. *Parodies from a Top Hat*, by Anni Weigand. Production and stage design: Anni Weigand. Puppets: Stuttgart youth clubs. Illustration: Male choir (cardboard tube puppets)

46 Harro Siegel Marionette Theatre, Brunswick. *Ti and Hapschisut*, by Richard Seewald. Production, puppets, and stage design: Harro Siegel. Music: Rudolf Konrad. Illustration: Three wealthy Egyptians

47 Harro Siegel Marionette Theatre, Brunswick. *The Double Head*, a grotesque play for marionettes by Wilhelm von Scholz. Production, puppets, and stage design: Harro Siegel. Illustration: The giant Columbus and Florinda, the lady without abdomen (marionettes)

48 Stuttgart Marionette Theatre. *Tiny Swift-Ball*, by Jan Malík. Puppets: Fritz Herbert Bross. Illustration: Grandmother (marionette)

49 "Die Hohnsteiner", Harald Schwarz stage, Essen (founded by Max Jacob). The *Magic Fiddle*, by Franz von Pocci. Production: Harald Schwarz. Puppets: Theo Eggink. Illustration: Cuprus, the spirit of the mountain

50 "Die Hohnsteiner", Friedrich Arndt stage, Hamburg (founded by Max Jacob). Illustration: Kasper, from the puppet play about Dr Faustus

51 Marionette studio of the State College of Visual Arts, Kassel. Studio experiments by a group of students. Production: Ernst Röttger. Puppets: Gerhard Hossner. Illustration: Haute école (marionettes)

52 "Die Hohnsteiner", Friedrich Arndt stage, Hamburg (founded by Max Jacob). *The Musical Carpet*, musical pantomime by a Hohnsteiner team. Production: Kurt Sydow. Puppets: Till Kock. Stage design: Karl-Heinz Cuno. Illustration: Robbers (glove puppets)

53 Marionette stage of the College for Art Education, Berlin. *The Play is Over*, by Jean-Paul Sartre. Production: Heinrich Amersdorffer. Puppets and stage design: work of students. Illustration: Figures (perspex marionettes)

54 Gerhards' Marionettes, Schwäbisch-Hall. *Lancelot and Sanderein*, an old Flemish play of courtly love, adapted by Fritz Gerhards. Production and puppets: Fritz Gerhards. Illustration: Lancelot and Sanderein (marionettes)

55 Kurt Sellier, Munich. *Marionette Cabaret*, by Kurt Sellier. Production, puppets and stage design: Kurt Sellier. Illustration: The lugubrious Herr Mäusespitz (marionette)

56 Hansjürgen Fettig Experimental Theatre, Stuttgart. *When Night Falls over Paris*, by Hansjürgen Fettig. Production, puppets, and stage design: Hansjürgen Fettig. Illustration: Max Besserschmier, the artist (rod puppet)

57 Studio G 12, Brunswick. *Scenes for Marionettes*, by Gottlieb Mordmüller and students. Production: Gottlieb Mordmüller. Puppets, stage design, and music: team of students. Illustration: Cutlery figure

58 Harry Kramer Mechanical Theatre, Berlin–Paris. *Thirteen Scenes*, an experiment with marionettes by Harry Kramer. Production and puppets: Harry Kramer. Music: Wolfgang Ramsbott. Illustration: Figure influenced by Kafka

59 "Die Klappe", Göttingen. *Dance of Death*, by Alfred Köhler. Production, puppets, and stage design: Alfred Köhler. Illustration: Harlequin and dancers

Italy

60 "I burattini della famiglia Ferrari" Theatre, Parma. A comedy by Giordano Ferrari. Puppets: Giordano Ferrari. First performance 1961. Illustration: Signora Adelaide

61 "Opera dei Burattini" Theatre, Rome. *Miraculous Things*, by Maria Signorelli. Puppets: Maria Signorelli. First performance 1947. Illustration: The old woman

62 Theatre of Cuticchio and Son, Palermo. Illustration: At Charlemagne's court ("Charlemagne's entry ... Long live the Emperor!")

Spain

63 Barcelona Marionette Theatre. *Danse triste*, by Jean Sibelius. Puppets: H. V. Tozer. Illustration: Death and the ballerina

Portugal

64 Branca-Flor Theatre, Lisbon. Puppets: Lilia da Fonseca. Illustration: Three marionettes which open, conclude, and comment on all the performances of this theatre: Pica-Pau, Brinca-Bem, and Branca-Flor (who gives her name to the theatre)

Austria

65 Richard Teschner, Vienna. Scene from *The Clock of Life* (from the puppet-theatre collection of the City of Munich)

66 Salzburg Marionette Theatre. *The Dying Swan*, by Camille Saint-Saëns. Illustration: Ballet study in memory of Anna Pavlova

67 Salzburg Marionette Theatre. *Eine kleine Nachtmusik*, by Wolfgang Amadeus Mozart. Illustration: Dance pantomime from the 1st Movement

68 Richard Teschner, Vienna. *Story of an Artist*. Illustration: Teschner's figures (from the puppet-theatre collection of the City of Munich)

German Democratic Republic

69 Carl Schröder, puppeteer, Dresden. *Iron Henry*, by Rudolph Thomas. Production and puppets: Carl Schröder. First performance 1962 (DEFA Cartoon Film Studio, Dresden). Illustration: Gustav, the co-operative executive

70 State Puppet Theatre, Dresden. *Kasper and the Truth Shawl*, by Peter Beckert, adapted from plays by Lena Foellbach. Production and puppets: Peter Beckert. First performance 1962

71 State Puppet Theatre, Dresden. *Duel with the Wolf*, by Georgi Landau. Production: Georg Liebe. Puppets: Achim Freyer. First performance 1963

72 Municipal Puppet Theatre, Karl-Marx-Stadt. *The Fairy Tale of Never-Never-Land*, by Mario Turra. Production: Peter Pillep. Puppets: Ruth Fischer. First performance 1964. Illustration: Inge and Atze

73 Carl Iwowski, puppeteer, Berlin. Illustration: Figure by Carl Iwowski (from the DEFA film *Pole Poppenspäler*, adapted from Theodor Storm)

74 German-Wendish Marionette Theatre, Bautzen. *How the Dragon of the Hadersberg was Defeated*, by B. Svaton. Production: Bert Ritscher. Puppets: Martin Schneider. First performance 1964

75 Oestreich-Ohnesorge Puppet Theatre, theatres of the city of Gera

76 Municipal Puppet Theatre, Magdeburg. *Laughter and Tears*, by S. Michalkow. Production: Gisela Wahlberg. Puppets: Hans Haupt. Stage design: Harry Bellmann. Music: Jochen Allihn. First performance 1963

77 Municipal Puppet Theatre, Magdeburg. *Caliph Stork*, adapted by Dieter Peust from Gertraude Röhricht. Production: Dieter Peust. Puppets: Hans Haupt. Stage design: Harry Bellmann. Music: Jochen Allihn

78 State Puppet Theatre, Dresden. *Big and Small Nicholas*, by Katharina Benkert. Production: Peter Beckert. Puppets: Andreas Reinhardt. First performance 1960

79 Carl Schröder, puppeteer, Dresden. *The Devil with the Three Golden Hairs*, by E. Jokusch. Production and puppets: Carl Schröder. First performance 1964 (DEFA Cartoon Film Studio, Dresden). Illustration: The robber

80 Carl Iwowski, puppeteer, Berlin. Illustration: Figures in the manner of Veit Stoss by Carl Iwowski (from the DEFA film *Pole Poppenspäler*)

81 As 70. *Kasper and the Truth Shawl*, by Peter Beckert, adapted from plays by Lena Foellbach. Production: Peter Beckert

82 Carl Schröder, puppeteer, Berlin. *Scapin's Pranks*, freely adapted from Molière by Klaus Eidam. Production and puppets: Carl Schröder. First performance 1965 (DEFA Cartoon Film Studio, Dresden)

83 "Die Böhlener", an amateur puppetry group of the Otto Grotewohl Works, Böhlen. *Puppet Revue*, by Siegfried Püffke and Franz Bauer. Production and puppets: Siegfried Püffke. First performance 1962

84 "Die Schatten", Fritz Gay's shadow theatre, Dresden. *The Blue Light*, by Fritz Gay. Production: Fritz Gay. Figures: Johannes Kühl. First performance 1960

85 "Die Schatten", Fritz Gay's shadow theatre, Dresden. *Little Two-Legs and the Horse*, by Margret Friskey. Production: Fritz Gay. Figures: Steffi Blum. First performance 1964

86 As 82. *Scapin's Pranks*, freely adapted from Molière by Klaus Eidam. Production: Carl Schröder

Poland

87 "Groteska" State Puppet Theatre, Cracow. *Threepenny Opera*, by Bertolt Brecht. Music: Kurt Weill. Translation: Bruno Winawer. Songs: Władysław Broniewski. Production: Zofia Jarema. Puppets: Lidia Minticz. Stage design: Kazimierz Mikulski

88 "Marcinek" State Puppet Theatre, Poznań. *The Little Tiger and the Pirates*, by H. Januszewska. Production: W. Wieczorkiewicz. Puppets and stage design: L. Serafinowicz and J. Berdyszak. First performance 1963. Illustration: The pirates

89 "Lalka" State Puppet Theatre, Warsaw. *Zwyrtala the Musician*, adapted from Kazimierz Przerwa-Tetmajer by Jan Wilkowski. Production: Jan Wilkowski. Puppets and stage design: Adam Kilian. Music: Krzysztof Penderecki. First performance 1958

90 State Puppet Theatre of Opole District. *The Legend of the Handsome Parysad*, by Bolesław Leśmian. Production: Jan Potisził. Puppets and stage design: Zygmunt Smandzik. Music: Jan Potisził. First performance 1958. Illustration: The children's nurse

91 As 89. *Zwyrtala the Musician*, adapted from Kazimierz Przerwa-Tetmajer by Jan Wilkowski. Production: Jan Wilkowski

92 "BAJ" State Puppet Theatre, Warsaw. *Shepherdess and Chimney Sweep*, adapted from Hans Andersen by Zbigniew Kopalko. Production: Zbigniew Kopalko. Puppets and stage design: Marian Stańczak. Music: Stanisław Prószyński

93 "Ateneum" State Puppet Theatre, Katowice. *Snow Legend*, by Milan Pavlik, translated by Irena Zitzman. Production, puppets, and stage design: Jerzy Zitzman

94 "Marcinek" State Puppet Theatre, Poznań. *A Ball at Professor Bączyński's House*, by K. I. Gałczyński. Mise-en-scène: L. Serafinowicz and W. Wieczorkiewicz. Production, puppets, and stage design: Leokadia Serafinowicz. Music: Franciszek Wasikowski

95 "Guliwer" State Puppet Theatre, Warsaw. *Adventure in Tiurtiulistan*, adapted from Wojciech Żukrowski by Joanna Gorczycka. Production: Monika Snarska. Puppets and stage design: Marian Stańczak. Music: Franciszek Wasikowski

96 As 89. Illustration: St Peter

97 "Lalka" State Puppet Theatre, Warsaw. *The Spellbound Horse*, adapted from B. Leśmian by Zbigniew Kopalko. Production: Zbigniew Kopalko. Puppets and stage design: Adam Kilian. First performance 1960. Illustration: The doctors

98 "Groteska" State Puppet Theatre, Cracow

99 "Miniatura" State Puppet Theatre, Gdańsk. *Bo w Mazurze taka dusza...* (from a Polish folk-song). Production: Natalia Gołębska and Michał Zarzecki. Puppets: Ali Bunsch. Stage design: Gizela Bachtin Karłowska

Soviet Union

100 State Central Puppet Theatre, Moscow. *The Divine Comedy*, by Isidor Stok. Production: S. Obraztsov and S. Samodur. Puppets and stage design: B. Tuzlukov. First performance 1962. Illustration: Adam and Eve

101 Kalinin Puppet Theatre. *The Inquisitive Little Elephant*, adapted from Rudyard Kipling's "The Elephant's Child" by E. Vladykhina. Production: I. Boyarsky. Puppets and stage design: K. Skaldina. First performance 1963. Illustration: The lion

102 State Central Puppet Theatre, Moscow. *Mine, mine alone*, by B. Tuzlukov. Production: S. Obraztsov and S. Samodur. Puppets and stage design: B. Tuzlukov. First performance 1958

103 Puppet Theatre, Kharkov. *Twelve Chairs*, adapted from I. Ilf and E. Petrov by M. Korolov. Production: V. Afanasiyev. Puppets: E. Goumenuke and E. Chegov. First performance 1960. Illustration: Mr Vorobyaninov

104 State Central Puppet Theatre, Moscow. Puppets by Sergei Obraztsov. Illustration: "Fill up the goblet" (from an old gipsy song)

105 Latvian Puppet Theatre, Riga. *Tip and Tap*, by E. Sterste. Production: T. Herzberg. Puppets: A. Nollendorf. Stage design: P. Shenhof. First performance 1961. Illustration: The twins Tip and Tap

106 Latvian Puppet Theatre, Riga. *The Wolf and the Kids*, by Y. Grabovsky. Production: T. Herzberg. Puppets: A. Nollendorf. Stage design: P. Shenhof. First performance 1961. Illustration: The kids

107 State Central Puppet Theatre, Moscow. Puppets: Sergei Obraztsov. Illustration: "We sat together" (song by Tchaikovsky)

108 State Central Puppet Theatre, Moscow. *A Visit at Chukovsky*. Illustration: The big and the small elephant

109 Estonian Puppet Theatre, Tallin. *Kalevipoeg's Journey to the End of the World*, after an Estonian epic. Production: F. Veike. Puppets: R. Laidre. First performance 1962

110 Bolshoi Puppet Theatre, Leningrad. *Cinderella*, by E. Schwarz. Production: M. Korolov. Puppets: B. Hovraleva. First performance 1963. Illustration: The king and the forester

111 Moscow Shadow Theatre. *Doctor Ibolit*, adapted from K. Chukovsky. Production: Em. May. Stage design: N. Tselikov. First performance 1963

112 Bolshoi Puppet Theatre, Leningrad. *First Two Points, Then Two Hooks*, by I. Skorospelov and N. Klykova. Production: E. Demmeni. Puppets and stage design: T. Bruny. First performance 1957. Illustration: The hero of the piece

113 Bolshoi Puppet Theatre, Leningrad. *Golden Paradise*, by J. and K. Čapek. Production: M. Korolov. Puppets: V. Malahieva. First performance 1960. Illustration: The crickets

Czechoslovakia

114 Puppetry Ensemble of the Czechoslovak Red Cross, Prague. *Fun and Games*. Puppets: Rudolf Zezula. First performance 1964

115 Špejbl and Hurvínek Theatre, Prague. Illustration: Špejbl and Hurvínek

116 Špejbl and Hurvínek Theatre, Prague. Performance by the theatre's team. Direction and puppets: Jan Dvořák. First performance 1963

117 Central Puppet Theatre, Prague. *Apollo and Hyacinthus*, by Wolfgang Amadeus Mozart. Production: Jan Malík. Puppets: Václav Havlík. First performance 1956

118 Central Puppet Theatre, Prague. *Immortal Laughter*, by Anton Chekhov. Production: Jan Malík. Puppets: Vojtěch Cinybulk. First performance 1954

119 Puppets' World Theatre, Prague. *Legend Law*, by K. Mašek fa Presto. Production, puppets, and stage design: Bohumír Koubek. First performance 1961

120 As 119

121 District Puppet Theatre, Ostrava. *The Enchanted Duckling*, by Maria Kann. Production: Jiří Jaros. Puppets: Václav Kábrt. First performance 1963. Illustration: Puppet representing the moon

122 "Radost" Puppet Theatre, Brno. *The Merchant*, by Vratislav Schilder. Production: Vratislav Schilder. Puppets: Ida Pullmannová

123 North Bohemian Puppet Theatre, Liberec. *The Story of the Terrible Dragon, the Princess, and the Cobbler*, by Maria Kownacka. Production: Oskar Batěk. Puppets: Josef Schmid. First performance 1962. Illustration: The witch Jaga and the tomcat

124 Amalgamated factory club at Bystřice, near Benešov. *King Lávra*, by K. Havlíček-Borovský. Production and décor: Zd. Jurena. First performance 1959. Illustration: King Lávra

125 As 123. Illustration: The horse

126 Alhambra Theatre. Prague. *Hold it—Cameras on Target!* by Ján Roháč, Milos Forman, and Jiří Středa. Production: Jiří Středa. Puppets: J. Procházka and Josef Lamka.

127 South Bohemian Puppet Theatre, České Budějovice. *Pale-Blue Peter*, by Urban Gyula. Production: Ladislav Dvořák. Puppets: L. Fridrich. First performance 1964. Illustration: The tomcat

128 State Puppet Theatre, Bratislava. *Little Atom, the Robot*, by Oldřich Augusta, translated by J. Ozábal. Production: Jan Chlebík. Puppets: B. Slavík. First performance 1963

129 Central Puppet Theatre, Prague. *The Divine Comedy*, by Isidor Stok. Production: Jan Malík and Erik Kolár. Puppets: Vojtěch Cinybulk. First performance 1962. Illustration: The Archangel Nicholas

130 West Bohemian Puppet Theatre, Karlovy-Vary (Karlsbad). *Unique Beauty*, by Yevgeniy Speranskiy. Production: Jindřich Halík. Puppets: Milada Bláhová. First performance 1961

131 Central Puppet Theatre, Prague. *Bajaja*, by František Pavlíček. Production: Jiří Jaroš. Puppets: Václav Havlík

132 Central Puppet Theatre, Prague. *The Nightingale*, by František Pavlíček. Production: Erik Kolár. Puppets: Richard Lander. First performance 1958. Illustration: The black Empress

Hungary

133 National Puppet Theatre, Budapest. *The Son of the White Horse*, by Géza Hegedüs. Production: Gyula Kovácz. Puppets and stage design: Vera Bródy. First performance 1963. Illustration: Two giants and the son of the white horse

134 National Puppet Theatre, Budapest. *The Successful Fool*, by T. Róna, Gy. Dénes, D. Szilágyi, and P. Tardos. Production: Kató Szönyi. Puppets: Vera Bródy. Stage design: Iván Koós. First performance 1960. Illustration: Hungarian dance

135 National Puppet Theatre, Budapest. *Toldi*, by Jànos Arany and Zoltán Jékely. Production: Kató Szönyi. Puppets: Vera Bródy. Stage design: Iván Koós. First performance 1963. Illustration: Miklós Toldi and his old servant in the steppe

136 National Puppet Theatre, Budapest. *The Sleeping Beauty*, by Ignác Rózsa. Production: Ildikó Kovács. Puppets: Vera Bródy. Stage design: György Sinóros-Szabó. First performance 1961

137 "Napsugár" Puppet Theatre, Békésczaba. *Dance Skit*. Production and puppets: Konrád Lenkefi. First performance 1963. Illustration: Dancing couple

138 As 134. Illustration. Musical comedy character on Mars

139 National Puppet Theatre, Budapest. *Aladdin and His Wonderful Lamp*, by Gernet, Bánd, and Devecseri. Production: Kató Szönyi. Puppets: Vera Bródy. Stage design: Iván Koós. First performance 1960. Illustration: The Grand Vizier and the sorcerer

140 National Puppet Theatre, Budapest. *A Midsummer Night's Dream*, by William Shakespeare, adapted by Dezsö Szilágyi. Pro-

duction: Kató Szönyi. Puppets: Vera Bródy. First performance 1964. Illustration: Hippolyta and Theseus

141 National Puppet Theatre, Budapest. *The Magic Tinderbox*, adapted by Dezsö Szilágyi from a story by Hans Andersen. Production: Kató Szönyi. Puppets: Vera Bródy. Stage design: György Sinóros-Szabó. First performance 1962. Illustration: The King and the jester

142 As 135. Illustration: The strange knight

143 As 140. Illustration: Character from *A Midsummer Night's Dream*.

144 Hungarian Television, Budapest. *Futrinka Street*, by Ágnes Bálint. Production: Márta Kende. Puppets: Saṅdor Lévai. First performance 1962. Illustration: The dog Morzsi

145 Puppet Theatre of the Cultural Centre of the Municipality of Pest. *The Little Lemon*, by Ede Tarbay. Production and puppets: Lajos Kos. First performance 1963. Illustration: Michou the squirrel

146 National Puppet Theatre, Budapest. *The Silver Flute*, by Dezsö Szilágyi. Production: Kató Szönyi and Anna Bánd. Puppets and stage design: Vera Bródy. First performance 1962. Illustration: The magic horse and the young peasant

147 As 140. Illustration: Oberon, ruler of the fairies

148 National Puppet Theatre, Budapest. *The Emperor's New Clothes*, adapted from Hans Andersen by Gy. Ránki. Production: Kató Szönyi. Puppets and stage design: Iván Koós. First performance 1961. Illustration: The Emperor

149 National Puppet Theatre, Budapest. *Michou the Squirrel goes on a Journey*, by J. Jenö Tersánszky and Gy. Kardos. Production: Gyula Kovács. Puppets and stage design: Vera Bródy. First performance 1961. Illustration: Michou the squirrel and Dr Begueteur (Mek-Mek) with the balloon

150 Group of marionette students, Debrecen. *In the Army*, by Mme Sándor Tóth. Production, puppets, and stage design: Mme Sándor Tóth. First performance 1963. Illustration: Scene with soldiers

Yugoslavia

151 *Ali Baba and the Forty Thieves*, by Zvonko Agbaba and Aleksandar Augustinčić. Production: Berislav Brajković. Stage design: Berislav Deželič. Illustration: The thief Pandža

152 *Tale of the Sea*, by Dusica Manojlović. Production: Marija Kulundžić. Choreography: Jelena Vajs. Puppets: Vukica Nikolin

153 *The Little Dog and the Little Cat*, adapted from Josef Čapek by Sreta Avrannović. Production: Zorka Festetić

154 "Pionir" Marionette Theatre, Split. *Beauty and the Beast*, by Vinko Protić. Production: Zvonko Kovač. Stage design: Vinko Protić

Rumania

155 Craiova Puppet Theatre. *Five Weeks in a Balloon*, adapted from Jules Verne by Anda Boldur. Production: Horia Davidescu. Stage design: Eustațiu Gregorian. First performance 1960

156 Jassy Puppet Theatre. *The ABC Emperor*, by Hanna and Josef Lamek. Production: Nicolae Brehnescu. Puppets and stage design: Rodica Șcraba and Aurelia Groapă. First performance 1963

157 "Tandarica" Marionette and Puppet Theatre, Bucharest. *The Baby Elephant*, adapted from Rudyard Kipling by Nina Cassian. Production: Stefan Lenkisch. Stage design: Mioara Buescu. First performance 1963

158 "Tandarica" Marionette and Puppet Theatre, Bucharest. *The Purse with Two Pennies*, adapted from Ion Creangă by Viorica Filipoiu. Production: Margareta Niculescu. Puppets: Ella Conovici. Stage design: Stefan Hablinski. First performance 1959. Illustration: The old gossip and the little chick

159 Brasov Puppet Theatre. *Let's Play*. Production: Bujor Rîpeanu. Stage design: Maria Dimitrescu. First performance 1962-63. Illustration: The little cockerel and the fox

160 Brasov Puppet Theatre. *The Tragedy of King Otakar and Prince Dalibor*, by George Călinescu. Production: Bujor Rîpeanu. Stage design: Maria Dimitrescu

161 "Tandarica" Marionette and Puppet Theatre, Bucharest. *I and Dead Matter*, by Mircea Crişan and Radu Stănescu. Production: Margareta Niculescu and Stefan Lenkisch. Puppets: Ella Conovici. Stage design: Mioara Buescu. First performance 1964

162 Brasov Puppet Theatre. Study for Vladimir Mayakovsky's *Bedbug*, by Elzevira Davidaovna. Stage design: Maria Dimitrescu

163 Brasov Puppet Theatre. *Cinderella*, adapted from Charles Perrault. Production: Jon Simionescu. Puppets and stage design: Maria Dimitrescu

164 "Tandarica" Marionette and Puppet Theatre, Bucharest. *The Book of Apollodorus*, by Gellu Naum. Production: Margareta Niculescu. Puppets: Ella Conovici. First performance 1962. Illustration: Mr Domilasolfa

165 As 161. *I and Dead Matter*, by Mircea Crişan and Radu Stănescu. Production: Margareta Niculescu and Stefan Lenkisch

166 Cluj Puppet Theatre. *Animal Tales*, adapted from Moricz Zsigmond by Ildikó Kovács. Production: Ildikó Kovács. Stage design: Edith Botar. First performance 1959

167 "Tandarica" Marionette and Puppet Theatre, Bucharest. *The Little Prince*, by Antoine de Saint-Exupéry, adapted by Letiţia Cîtza. Production: Radu Penciulescu. Puppets and stage design: Stefan Hablinski. First performance 1960

168 "Tandarica" Marionette and Puppet Theatre, Bucharest. Illustration: The puppet Tandarica. Puppeteer: Dorina Tanasescu

169 "Tandarica" Marionette and Puppet Theatre, Bucharest. *The Heroic Deeds of Gallant Hercules*, adapted from Greek mythology by Al. Mitru. Production: Stefan Lenkisch. Puppets: Ella Conovici. First performance 1959. Illustration: Eurystheus

170 "Tandarica" Marionette and Puppet Theatre, Bucharest. *Dr Doolittle*, by V. Korostiliov. Production: Stefan Lenkisch. Puppets: Ella Conovici. First performance 1960. Illustration: The robber Barmalei

171 "Tandarica" Marionette and Puppet Theatre, Bucharest. *A Train has Left*, adapted from Gianni Rodari by Stefan Iureş and Ira Vrabie. Production: Nicolae Massim. Stage design, masks, and costumes: Ella Conovici. First performance 1962

172 "Tandarica" Marionette and Puppet Theatre, Bucharest. *Pacala*, a popular play by Brînduşa-Zaiţa-Silvestru. Production: Stefan Lenkisch. Puppets: Ioana Constantinescu. First performance 1959. Illustration: The Boyar and Ileana

173 Oradea Puppet Theatre. *Harap Alb*, adapted from Ion Creangă by Nella Stroescu. Production: Francisca Mirişan. Puppets and stage design: Paul Fuchs. First performance 1963. Illustration: The old man, the Emperor, and Harap Alb

Bulgaria

174 Central Puppet Theatre, Sofia. *Cinderella*. Production: Silyana Dotcheva. Puppets: Lilyana Angelova. Stage design: Lilyana Angelova, realized by Ivan Zonev

175 State Puppet Theatre, Burgas. *The Wonderful Candy*, by Mikhail Korabelnik. Production: Sergei Vissonov. Stage design: Dora Nikolava. Illustration: The dog Topsik

176 Municipal Puppet Theatre, Sofia. *Puss in Boots*, by Vladimir Bonev. Production: Sergei Vissonov. Stage design and puppets: Irina Leiséva

177 Plovdiv Puppet Theatre. *Holidays*, by Boris Akhchiysky and Ljuben Bojadjier. Production: Aleko Minchev. Stage design: Boris Akhchiysky

178 Touring Puppet Theatre, Sofia. *Puss in Boots*, by Nina Stoicheva. Production: Sergei Vissonov. Stage design: Irina Leiséva

179 Varna Puppet Theatre. *Dr Doolittle*, by Lilyana Dotcheva and Dimiter Dimitrov. Production: Ivan Ovanov and Georgi Bachvarov. Stage design: Georgi Bachvarov. Illustration: The singer

180 Central Puppet Theatre, Sofia. *Peter and the Wolf*, by Sergei Prokofiev. Production: Athanas Ilkov and Nikolina Georgieva. Stage design and puppets: Yordanka Licheva. Realized by Ivan Zonev. Illustration: The huntsman and Peter

181 As 180. Illustration: Grandfather

Greece

182 Athens Puppet Theatre. *The Young Master of Castoria*, a Macedonian folk-tale adapted by Helene Theochari-Peraki. Production and puppets: Helene Theochari-Peraki. Stage design: Anthoula Xanthou. First performance 1958. Illustration: The young master, the good princess, the proud princess

183 Athens Puppet Theatre. *Each in His Own Way*, a Greek folk-tale adapted by Helene Theochari-Peraki. Production and puppets: Helene Theochari-Peraki. Stage design: Anthoula Xanthou. First performance 1962. Illustration: The old man, the old woman

Canada

184 George Merten, Toronto. *Beauty and the Beast*, by George and Elizabeth Merten. First performance 1954. Illustration: Three Siskers marionettes (now in the Detroit Art Museum)

185 George Merten, Toronto. Illustration: Two workmen (glove puppets)

United States of America

186 Illustration: Jim Henson's "Moppets"

187 Illustration: Puppets by George Latshaw, Ohio

188 Bill Baird's Marionettes, New York City. Illustration: Pipgrass

189 As 188. Illustration: Snarky and Heathcliff

190 Illustration: Knight on horseback, by Benjamin Blake, Boston

Cuba

191 National Puppet Theatre, Havana. *The Sad Widow*, by José Brene. Puppets: Pepe Camejo. Stage design: Armando Morales. First performance 1963

192 Instituto Cubano de Arte e Industria Cinema (ICAIC), Havana. *Valo-Valo*. Scenario: Miguel Fleitas. Production: Miguel Fleitas. Puppets: Juan García. Stage design: Orlando Torres. Music: Armando de Sequeira. First performance 1963

Brazil

193 Brazilian Society of Puppeteers. *A Nau Catarineta*, a folklore subject dramatized by Cecilia Meirelles. Production: Anisio Medeiros. Stage design: Olga Obry. Music: Luiz Cosme

Argentina

194 Popular Marionette Theatre, Buenos Aires. *The Play of Dr Faustus*, by Javier Villafañe. Production, puppets, and stage design: Ariel Bufano. First performance 1950

195 Touring Puppet Theatre, Buenos Aires. *The Death of Pulcinella*, by Juan Gelman. Production: Ariel Bufano and Sergio de Cecco. Puppets: Marta Gavensky and Beatriz Suárez. First performance 1962

Israel

196 "Bubatron" Puppet Theatre, Kibbutz of Givat-Chaim. *King of the Desert*, by Honso (David Ben-Shaldom). Illustration: The good dwarf

197 As 196. Illustration: Ziva, one of the kibbutz children

Turkey

198 Shadow puppets. Illustration: Karagöz and Hadjewad (from the State Puppet Theatre Collection, Dresden)

Iran

199 *Pahlevan Kachal* (Pulchinello), an Iranian folk-tale adapted by Djennati. Puppets: Marian Khodadad, Mohtaram Sobbi, Shahrbanou Partovi, and Roshanak Partovi. Stage design: Parviz Kardan

200 Various traditional Iranian marionette characters. They do not tell a story, but represent different spectacles such as wrestling, dancing, etc.

United Arab Republic (Egypt)

201 Cairo Puppet Theatre. Illustration: Scene from *Shebab el Din's Donkey* (Guest performance in Berlin, 1964)

202 Cairo Puppet Theatre. *Shebab el-Din's Donkey*, by Salah Ghahin. Production: Nagy Shaker and Ibrahim Salem. Puppets: Nagy Shaker. Stage design: Moustafa Kamel. Music: Sayed Mekawy. First performance 1962

203 As 202

India

204 "Darpan" Drama School, Ahmedabad. *Savitri-Satyavan*, a shadow play adapted by Meher Rustom Contractor. Production and puppets: Meher Rustom Contractor. Illustration: from Scene 1

205 As 204. Illustration: from Scene 8

206 As 204. Illustration: from Scene 4

207 As 204. Illustration: from Scene 5

Contents

Acknowledgments for Illustrations

Alpha–Omega, France 19; Amateur photograph printed by Foto-Mann, Gera 75; Amati and Bettati, Parma 60; Anand Studio, India 204–207; Albrecht Antowne, Cairo 202, 203; Associated Press, Brussels 27; Branko Balić, Zagreb 151; Beata Bergström, Sweden 39; Idöapó Birodalma, Hungary 136; Fritz Herbert Bross, Bad Cannstadt 48; Jan Bussell, Egham 13; Consejo Nacional de Cultura, Cuba 191; André Cornet, France 20; Peter Croydon, Toronto 185; Karl-Heinz Cuno, Laiz-Donau 52; Hans Derks, Maastricht 34, 35; Marian Domisse, 's-Gravenhage 32; Zdenek Dukát, Prague 114; David Eldan, Israel 196, 197; Gretl Eschenlohr, Mattsee 66, 67; Foto-Schurig, Remscheid-Lennep 49; Fövárosi-Foto, Budapest 139; Seiji Fujishiro, Japan 238; Gareth, London 10; Fritz Gerhards, Schwäbisch-Hall 54; Claus Gräwe, Hamburg 50; Hacquart, Amiens 22; E. Hartwig, Poland 91; Heinrich Heidersberger, Brunswick 46, 47; College for Visual Arts, Kassel 51; T. E. Howard, England 1; Raymond Irons, England 2; Taiji Kawajiri, Japan 229, 230, 233; Éva Keleti, Budapest 133-135, 138, 140-143, 146-148; Kesenian, Indonesia 224, 226, 227; Hoang Kim, Vietnam 208-210; Alan Kimber, England 12; Alfred Köhler, Göttingen 59; Cuban Institute of Film Art and Film Production (ICAIC) 192; W. S. Lanchester, England 6; B. Lecoutre, France 17; Tadeusz Link, Poland 99; Jan Malík, Prague 211-219, 222, 223; Gérard Marinier, France 24; Albert Marrion, Liverpool 8; Barbara Meffert, Berlin 73, 80, 201; George Merten, Toronto 184; Kiichi Mimura, Japan 232; Gottlieb Mordmüller, Brunswick 57; Franciszek Myszkowsk, Warsaw 92, 95; Tadao Nagahama, Japan 234; Margret Noske, Berlin 53; Olga Obry, Brazil 193; Ohidy, France 25; Jaroslav Paulus, Liberec 123; Bedřich Pešek, Prague 126; V. Philpott, England 3, 9, 11; Photo Contact, Belgium 26; Paul M. Pietzsch, Rome 61; Podhorský, Czechoslovakia 128; Robert Poisneau, France 23; Viktor Radnický, Czechoslovakia 121, 122, 131, 132; Wolfgang Ramsbott, Berlin 58; Renard, France 21; Cliff Riddle, Hollywood 190; Archiv Albrecht Roser, Stuttgart 43, 44; Yoshikatsu Saeki, Japan 236, 237; Chris Sandman, Helsinki 42; Vladislav Scholz, Czechoslovakia 117; Carl Schröder, Dresden 69-72, 74, 78, 79, 81-83, 86, 198, 228; Kurt Sellier, Munich 55; Atelier Spelthahn, Magdeburg 76, 77; H. P. Seufert, Waiblingen 56; Helmut Spisla, Suhl 84, 85; Hans Steiner, Switzerland 31; Karel Stoll, Prague 118, 124; Alo Storz, Stuttgart 45; Sturlason, Norway 36, 37; T. Sumiński, Poland 98; Fény Szöv, Budapest 137, 145, 149; Yuichiro Tamura, Japan 235; Richard Tomasi, Austria 65, Mme Sándor Tóth, Debrecen 150; Miroslav Tuma, Prague 127; Mary Turner, England 4; Ulkoja, Amsterdam 32; Nándor Urbán, Budapest 144; Pavel Vácha, Prague 119, 120; Elisa da Conceição Veríssimo, Lisbon 64; Jean Villiers, Paris 16; Frans Vink, 's-Gravenhage 33; At. Vladenov, Bulgaria 180; Hylton Warner, England 5; Michael Wolgensinger, Zurich 29, 30; Julius Wolski, Cracow 87; G. Wyszomirska, Poland 94; Alexander Young, England 7; Czesław Zieliński, Katowice 93.

14